Law Firm Fees &
Compensation:
Value & Growth Dynamics

A LawBiz® Management
Special Report

by **Edward Poll**

Published by

LawBiz® Management Company
(a division of Edward Poll & Associates, Inc.)
421 Howland Canal
Venice, CA 90291
Phone: (800) 837-5880
Fax: (310) 578-1769
E-mail: EdPoll@LawBiz.com
Web site: www.LawBiz.com
Weblog: www.LawBizblog.com

Report design by Creative Quadrant, Inc.
Illustrations by Simmie Williams Illustrations.

Nothing contained in this publication is to be considered as the
offering of management advice or legal advice for specific cases, and
readers are responsible for obtaining such counsel from their own
advisers. This publication and any forms, suggestions or advice herein
are intended for educational and informational purposes only.

Additional copies of this publication may be purchased from Edward
Poll & Associates, Inc., which also produces other publications of
interest to the legal and professional services communities. Discounts
are available for bulk orders.

The Business of Law® is a registered trademark of
Edward Poll & Associates, Inc.

Library of Congress Control Number: 2008903141

ISBN: 978-0-9654948-9-2

Dedication

To my team, to the many mentors and influencers, who have made my life blessed. There are too many to list, but you are alive and well in all of my being.

Table of Contents

Table of Contents *continued*

Foreword

When I founded "AdamSmithEsq.com" over four years ago, one of my motivations was that I believed there was a tremendous need for an online publication and forum discussing the strategy and economics of large law firms—and I couldn't find anything on target. Today, with the readership of "AdamSmithEsq.com" global, it seems that surmise was correct. With *Law Firm Fees & Compensation: Value & Growth Dynamics,* Ed Poll is filling a similar void for law practices of all sizes. There is nothing out there as comprehensive and thorough, or as practical and down to earth, as this guide to every material issue about how law firms charge for their services and collect their fees.

Ed covers a range of critical topics, including:
- Hourly billing, its history and genesis
- The engagement letter, including ethical considerations surrounding it
- Budgets and time, pricing, and scope
- Trust accounts and the special professional and ethical obligations appurtenant to them
- "Value" billing, including alternative pricing methods such as blended hourly rates, fixed or flat fees, contingency or percentage fees, premium pricing, retainers, and combinations of these methods
- Refunded fees and split "ownership" of matters and fees (often between a lawyer and his or her firm)
- The nuts and bolts of billing, including collections

Lastly, Ed rounds out the picture by discussing how fees and billing intersect with and dynamically influence internal firm issues of compensation, as well as two of the most powerful external waves building force and soon to roll ashore on the cozy beaches of law firms: (1) commoditization and (2) convergence.

In short, if you help manage a law firm of any size—from your own solo practice to a department or practice area at a large firm—you will find clear-headed advice from Ed's nearly two decades of experience helping lawyers manage the business side of their practices more effectively.

And that's the theme of this publication, isn't it?

Lawyers—take it from me, I'm one!—frequently are allergic to the notion that their firms *are* businesses. And Ed's message? "Get over it."

Ignoring the business dimensions of one's practice cannot only be dangerous to your income, it can alienate clients and colleagues alike, impede your own professional success, and diminish your future potential. So what does being "businesslike" mean? It's nothing frightening in the least—but you must do the following:

- Manage cases and transactional assignments like projects. That's what they are. There's a reason corporate America has refined "project management" to a science.
- Recognize that your individual success comes within the context of the firm, and that its success and yours are two sides of the same coin.
- Finally, why not emulate corporations more explicitly? In serving your clients, these must be your priorities:
  - Communicate, communicate, communicate.
  - Be driven by the highest standards of client service.
  - Be a team player inside your firm and with your client. Your highest success will come in league with your firm's success and your client's.

Ed Poll enthusiastically espouses these principles throughout this new publication—and he provides detailed advice on how to put them into action in your law practice.

> —Bruce MacEwen
> New York City
> March 2008

About the Author

Edward Poll, J.D., M.B.A., CMC, is a nationally recognized coach, certified management consultant, author, and speaker on law practice management topics. Ed's mission and passion is to make attorneys and law firms more effective in serving their clients, more efficient in delivering their services, and more profitable.

Ed has the unique blend of 25 years of law practice (including civil litigation and corporate/business law) and more than 17 years of helping lawyers become better at The Business of Law® and, thus, more profitable. He also was the CEO and COO of several manufacturing businesses.

He is the author of numerous articles and books that demonstrate how to successfully manage a law practice, among them *Attorney and Law Firm Guide to the Business of Law,* 2nd Edition, and *Collecting Your Fee: Getting Paid from Intake to Invoice,* both published by the American Bar Association. Other works include *Secrets of The Business of Law®: Successful Practices for Increasing Your Profits, MORE Secrets of The Business of Law®: Ways to Be More Effective, Efficient, and Profitable, The Profitable Law Office Handbook: A Guide to Successful Business Planning,* and *Selling Your Law Practice: The Profitable Exit Strategy,* all published by LawBiz.® He has also created the LawBiz® Management Special Report Series, which includes *Business Competency for Lawyers, The Successful Lawyer-Banker Relationship, Disaster Preparedness & Recovery Planning for Law Firms,* and now *Law Firm Fees & Compensation.*

In addition, Ed taught "Creating New Business Enterprises" in the Department of Entrepreneurship, University of California, Los Angeles (UCLA), and created the "Business of Law Practice" for the University of Southern California (USC) Law Center for Advanced Professional Education, among other programs.

He is also a leader in the California and national bar associations. Ed has served on boards of various local, state, and national bar associations, including as Chair of the State Bar of California's Law Practice Management & Technology Section and as a member of the Council of the American Bar Association Law Practice Management Section. He is a Fellow of the College of Law Practice Management and most recently was inducted as one of only five charter members to the Million Dollar Consultant Hall of Fame.

Section 1:

Cost Versus Value: The Rise of the Hourly Rate

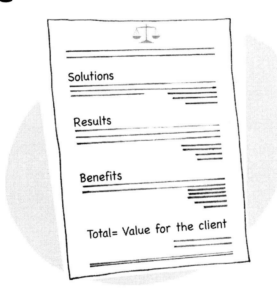

Solutions

Results

Benefits

Total= Value for the client

Historically, until well into the post-World War II era, legal fees were based primarily on the nature of the service provided, the results achieved, and the amount at stake.

Determining an appropriate fee for the work was a matter of professional judgment.

That changed in the mid-1960s when clients began demanding detailed billing statements and lawyers implemented timekeeping records as a management tool to seek greater efficiencies. As a result, today most lawyers are paid by the hour—almost in the same way as an hourly laborer. When lawyers are paid by the number of hours worked, though, self-interest can and often does affect their judgment about how much work to do for the client. Most lawyers' billings are "features" lists: This is what I did, this is the amount of time it took to do it, and this is what you owe me. That approach breeds dissatisfaction among clients because it doesn't address value and benefits—the worth to the client, as opposed to the cost of the service.

Negative Impacts of Hourly Rates

There are two fundamental considerations involved in evaluating the ways in which professional services can, and should, be billed:

- ▸ Any billing method that does not depend exclusively on time spent as a measure of value provides an incentive for efficiency and early resolution of the matter being handled.

- ▸ The value of legal services and the quality of those services, both as perceived by the client, are the defining characteristics of effective billing. From the viewpoint of clients, they are buying favorable solutions, results, and benefits—not time.

These two factors explain why the successful law firm of the future will *not* use straight hourly rates to bill for its services.

In fact, studies and surveys have already exhaustively demonstrated that clients, especially business clients, are fundamentally rejecting hourly rates as a valid billing gauge for legal services, with that rejection centering on eight key concerns:

- ▸ Perceived abuse in terms of overbilling

- ▸ Lack of predictability in the overall costs of the matter

- ▸ Lack of control over the factors involved in setting the bill

- ▸ Discouragement of efficiency

- ▸ Discouragement of value-added services

- ▸ Disconnect with technological efficiencies

- ▸ Inequality in hours spent delivering the same services

- ▸ Discouragement of risk and benefit sharing

The sum of these objections is that hourly rates reflect neither (1) the actual costs that go into the provision of legal services nor (2) the value that clients perceive in those services.

The hourly rate is also the focal point of other pernicious effects on The Business of Law®. Take, for example, its impact on four areas: client communication, firm governance, lawyer succession, and, ironically, firm financial performance.

Let's consider each of these four areas in turn.

Client Communication

Lawyers who are intent on piling up billable hours tend to focus on the task at hand without communicating to the client exactly what work they are doing. Such lawyers may be doing a great job dealing with documents, the court, and the opposing party, but because the client doesn't hear about these things, the lawyer fails to build up the client's confidence and trust. So ultimately, no matter how successful the end result is, the client doesn't understand what has been accomplished and may even refuse to pay the bill when it comes due. Clients appreciate communication—and the more, the better. But when client communication is just another itemized function charged by the hour, both lawyer and client lose focus on the real intent—which is building a relationship, not creating a new charge.

Firm Governance

Many states require that partners and other lawyers with managerial authority in a law firm must take reasonable measures to ensure that all lawyers in the firm conform to the Rules of Professional Conduct. (See, e.g., Rule 5.1 of the ABA Model Rules of Professional Conduct.) Some states either provide for or are considering providing that lawyers who have managerial responsibility within a firm are *personally* responsible when others in the firm violate the rules or are negligent in their performance of legal services. This is a heavy burden that many lawyers fail to attend to because they incline toward focusing only on rainmaking and their own billable hours. This leaves a lot of room for error by others who are essentially

The Defining Characteristics of Effective Billing:

- The value of legal services as perceived by the client
- The quality of those services as perceived by the client

going unsupervised, thus increasing the risks of personal responsibility for lawyers with managerial authority over negligent colleagues.

Lawyer Succession

In many law firms, the older partners run the "business" side of the practice while the younger lawyers tend to be the followers. Because law firm compensation is generally based on hourly billing output, senior partners may not want to share information about clients or prospects with a next-generation lawyer, owing to fear the younger lawyer might "steal" business before the first lawyer is ready to step away from active practice. This creates a problem of client service continuity as older lawyers retire.

Financial Performance

Lawyers often think that financial success means ever-rising billable hours. The truth is that a lawyer's inventory is not billable (or billed) hours—instead, it is the cash those hours represent. Uncollected billables are a financial liability that, at worst, can sink a firm.

More than one law firm has been forced to file for bankruptcy even though it had substantial sums in outstanding accounts receivable. Had these firms been more diligent and aggressive in collecting the money owed for outstanding billed and unbilled work-in-progress (WIP) hours, they could have remained alive.

An Integrated Approach: The Three-Point Intersect

Law firms mirror their clients in business terms. To the extent that law firms provide the services their clients need, at a price the clients are willing to pay, firms will grow. Otherwise, they will be challenged to stay in business.

Every law firm is a business. And every business has three common elements: Get the work (sales); do the work (production); and get paid (finance). Where these three elements intersect for lawyers is what I call the location of The 3-Dimensional Lawyer™. When this intersection is achieved, the lawyer's practice, and therefore the lawyer, is in balance—in harmony. With effective communications between lawyer and client, it is in this balanced state that the client is well served and truly values the lawyer's efforts; the lawyer both enjoys the client and is challenged by the matter; and the client promptly pays the bill.

To achieve this balance, lawyers need to understand their own business operations better than they typically do. This understanding centers on the interaction between what law firms charge clients for their services, how effectively they collect their

The 3-Dimensional Lawyer™

fees from clients, and how lawyers themselves are compensated for the work they bill. The goal of this understanding should be to create an effective way of measuring, billing, and collecting the value of services provided.

Ensuring any firm's business success requires taking an integrated approach to the issues of fees, billing, collection, and compensation. This LawBiz® Special Report outlines the basics of such an approach. The key elements include:

> ▶ A written engagement letter that sets forth the clients' obligations and responsibilities, including the paying of their bills

Clients appreciate communication—and the more, the better. But when client communication is just another itemized function charged by the hour, both lawyer and client lose focus on the real intent—which is building a relationship, not creating a new charge.

- ► A budget for events, time, and money so that clients are not surprised by what is billed but instead buy into and accept it

- ► Billing methods that are easy to understand and clearly list actions taken on the client's behalf while relating the actions to the time it took to realize value, making the bill more meaningful to the client

- ► Clear delineation of value realized by the client

- ► Frequent communication to ensure that an actual or perceived problem does not result in a client deciding not to pay a bill

- ► Collection processes that create a formal system to secure client payment without delay or contention

- ► Compensation systems that recognize the contribution of the individual lawyer as well as the best business interests of the firm as a whole

The Ultimate Objective

Our objective as lawyers is to help people's lives improve. In the course of fulfilling that objective, we should provide and account for our services in such a way that clients understand the value as well as the cost of what we do. When that happens, fees are not an issue and client complaints do not occur. When that doesn't happen, lawyers are at best seen as a necessary but expensive evil.

The goal of this LawBiz® publication is to help lawyers and law firms run their practices in a more businesslike way that will improve the professionalism of the practice of law. The purpose is not simply to get more money for the lawyer; it is also to benefit the client. A profitable practice is much more likely to avoid ethical problems such as dipping into client trust accounts, either as direct fraud or as a stopgap "loan." Moreover, a law firm run as a business will also approach client service more efficiently—returning phone calls promptly, creating and adhering to a budget, providing sufficient details on clients' invoices, and effectively providing and conveying value. That, ultimately, is the true meaning of The Business of Law®.

Section 2:

The Engagement Letter: Essential Issues

I t is a fundamental business and professional necessity that lawyers have a signed engagement letter for both new clients and existing clients, stating each party's responsibilities for making the engagement a success. You will have a much easier time meeting your client's expectations and collecting your fee if you incorporate all essentials into the engagement letter. Moreover, the engagement letter is your prime opportunity to make sure that clients understand that they are entering into a two-way relationship: The lawyer agrees to perform to the best of his or her ability in accordance with professional standards, and the client agrees to communicate and cooperate fully—which includes paying the bill.

Knowing the Client's Matter

It is critical to gain an understanding of the client's matter before settling on the way the firm wants to charge for the services it will provide. This requires establishing a process that you can go through with the client for determining goals and tracking progress on the matter. Here is an example of the steps such a process could include:

- ► Identification of goals to be achieved for the client

- ► Current status of the project or case

- ► Complexity of the project or case

- ► Number and description of the parties involved

- ► Documents to be generated (including drafting responsibility and expected number of drafts)

- ► Extent of travel anticipated

- ► Extent of work to be done by in-house counsel and outside counsel respectively

- ► Extent of expected negotiations and discovery

Results You Can Expect When You Build an Effective Two-Way Relationship with Clients

Profit
Happy clients pay their bills.

Revenue
Happy clients bring new business.

Effectiveness
You build a caring bond with clients.

Counselor
You become the lead adviser for clients in many other matters.

Protection
Client satisfaction is the best protection against malpractice claims.

▸ Staffing plan for the firm and other professionals involved

This entire process aims to obtain as much information as possible about the client's goals and expectations. Information should cover parties, issues, anticipated strategies, and desired outcomes. Understanding the client's objectives is critical to defining the payment obligations for the engagement.

Terms of the Engagement

Getting fees and payment terms in writing is at the heart of the engagement letter. Before beginning an engagement, you should get the client's written agreement regarding the fee to be charged and how it will be calculated, when the fee is to be paid, and the consequences of nonpayment, including the lawyer's right to withdraw, provided the client is not prejudiced, in accordance with the rules of your jurisdiction. This increases the chances of collecting your fee significantly because the client understands what to expect. At a minimum, the following terms should be covered in the engagement letter, with both lawyer and client stipulating and agreeing to the facts stated:

- ▶ Who the lawyer is representing

- ▶ The name of the responsible attorney

- ▶ The scope of the representation—i.e., what the lawyer will and will not do

- ▶ The fee to be charged and how it will be calculated. (Recommendation: Insert an initial stamp in the margin by this paragraph and have both client and attorney initial their understanding and acceptance of the provision.)

- ▶ When the fee is to be paid (Recommendation: Use an initial stamp as above.)

- ▶ The consequences of nonpayment, including the lawyer's right to withdraw if the client fails

Understanding the client's objectives is critical to defining the payment obligations for the engagement.

to honor his or her obligations under the terms of the agreement

► Budgeting and staffing

► Frequency and method of communications from lawyer to client

► The client's responsibilities, including payment in accordance with the agreement

► Dispute resolution procedures if either party to the engagement has a dispute with the other

► Resolution of conflicts of interest or other ethical issues

► Description of the firm's file retention policy, and the client's acceptance of the return of his or her original documents and files upon termination of the representation

This list is heavily weighted to the financial side, and for good reason: Stipulating payment rates and terms up front is the best way to get paid. There are additional considerations that bear on this from both the attorney and the client side, including:

- Identification of the clients, and if appropriate, identification of who are not clients

- Naming, if appropriate, the client or third party who is responsible for paying the attorney's bills

- The responsible attorney the client can call

- The authorized client representative, if applicable

- Legal services specifically excluded, such as related litigation or appellate work

- Specific client communication responsibilities, such as keeping the attorney current with address changes

- Definition of the attorney fee model (such as hourly, fixed, or contingent)

- Specific client approval if there is to be a division of fees between non-firm attorneys, recognizing the fact that most states require written client approval of fee-sharing agreements between attorney firms

This process of detailing and negotiating to prepare the engagement letter enables you to avoid a client who has unrealistic expectations or demands or who might believe that your estimates, whether of time or outcome or costs, are guarantees instead of informed estimates. Discussing engagement terms also will frequently uncover the client who will in the future express irritation with delay, who will chronically complain about everything, who will demand constant or instant attention, or who expects abnormal handholding.

Means of Payment: Special Points about Credit Cards

All lawyers should consider accepting credit cards for payment, as a convenience for both parties. Many people today rely on plastic and therefore paying legal bills with credit cards may be easier for them. One of the benefits to the client of paying with a credit card is that there may be roughly a six-month window in which to raise a dispute and request the credit card company reverse the charge. However, payment for a subsequently disputed legal bill may require the lawyer to place a like amount in a client's trust account. At worst, the credit card company could reverse the charge, credit the customer, and debit the law firm.

Accordingly, be sure to spell out in your original engagement letter whether credit cards will be accepted in payment. If they will, stipulate how the card will be used and have clients sign an authorization to charge their cards. Send a copy of the authorization along with your bill. Use client payments by credit card only for legal services rendered. They should *not* be requested or accepted for unearned retainers or charge-backs of unearned fees unless your jurisdiction permits it. You may want to secure the client's agreement that no dispute with the law firm will be raised with or adjudicated by the credit card company. In other words, the client agrees that the charge is nonrefundable and cannot be reversed by the credit card company. With such a statement in hand, the credit card company is likely not to become the arbiter of a dispute with a client. Any dispute over fees paid by credit card should be settled between the lawyer and the client, governed by the Rules of Professional Conduct. Check your state rules to determine the optional and mandatory procedures to settle fee disputes. However, review Regulation Z—the Federal Reserve regulation implementing the consumer credit protections of the Truth-in-Lending Act of 1968—which seems to say that it is a federal offense to prevent credit card companies from reversing a disputed charge.

Other Fee Considerations

Because the engagement letter is the foundation for all future fee and collection considerations, never hesitate to be as detailed as possible in the terms spelled out. The following considerations typify the types of collection problems that an effective engagement letter can proactively address.

The importance of a written fee agreement. In some states the Rules of Professional Conduct require a written fee agreement for contingency work but not for hourly or transactional work. Many states are moving in the direction of requiring written agreements for all engagements. But even beyond that, many attorneys miss a real opportunity by not having a written fee agreement. There are distinct marketing benefits for the practice in terms of defining and managing client expectations *and* how these expectations will be met, as well as removing uncertainty about fees.

Special considerations that apply to trust funds. Lawyers should provide in their engagement letters that the client authorizes the lawyer to debit client trust account funds after a reasonable time from the date of billing. The client will retain the right to dispute the charges, although he or she is unlikely to do so if you both agree on the need to be timely with any objections. Communication is a two-way boulevard and such an approach preserves the rights of both clients and lawyers.

Specify your collection cycle. Set specific dates of the month by which each client will be billed, being sure to stagger the billing dates across your client list—by, for example, billing one-fourth of the alphabet each week. You will thereby receive money from one-fourth of your clients weekly, rather than from all clients once per month. This evens out your receipt of cash over the month. You could also shorten your monthly billing cycle by spelling out in the engagement letter that invoices will be mailed out on or about the 25th of the month so that clients receive statements on or before the first day of the following month. Since most businesspeople close their payable cycles on the first to the fifth of the month, and pay their bills on or about the tenth to the fifteenth of the month, a bill that comes after the tenth is frequently kept for payment until the following month.

Sample Engagement Letter Provisions

The appendix to this report gives examples of wording for the types of fee provisions that may be contained in the letters of engagement for various types of work:

hourly and contingency, litigation and nonlitigation. These examples are not meant to be all-inclusive. They do demonstrate, however, the types of specifics that an engagement letter may include. The lesson to be drawn from them is that, rather than leave any doubt in a client's mind about the terms of the engagement, it is always better to be explicit and detailed in the letter's provisions. Remember, law firms are not the victims of their delinquent clients. Firms themselves cause collection problems by failing to tell clients at the outset what is expected from them and also failing to do follow-ups about maintaining those expectations.

Section 3:

Budgets for Client Matters

A ll companies do some type of business planning, although the form and components of the plan can vary widely. Global multinational companies generate and monitor very detailed written plans, while the plan of a smaller business may exist largely in the entrepreneur's head. But whether you're making widgets or providing professional services, operating according to a budget is the essence of a successful plan.

Too often, lawyers tend to dismiss the importance—or even the practicality—of preparing a budget, especially for client matters. Typically there are three reasons for this:

1. They believe that their services in a matter will depend on too many unforeseen variables—for example, what motions opposing counsel will file or what problems might turn up during discovery.

2. They want to excel at what they do, whether it's negotiating a deal, drafting a contract, or litigating. They don't want the quality of their services to be constrained by budget limitations.

3. To some extent, they fear that budgeting for a matter is merely a client strategy to reduce the fees the client is willing to pay.

Why Develop a Budget?

In reality, preparing a budget at the start of any matter ensures greater productivity and cost-effectiveness for both sides. A budget is merely an estimate of what the parties expect to happen. The lawyer should not strive for the highest possible fee, and the client should not attempt to get the cheapest lawyer in town.

Creating a budget shows clients—whether they are individuals, small businesses, or corporate counsel—that you are sensitive to their needs. In addition, it

Creating a budget shows clients—whether they are individuals, small businesses, or corporate counsel—that you are sensitive to their needs. In addition, it reinforces that you are providing a valuable service and not just a block of hourly time.

reinforces that you are providing a valuable service and not just a block of hourly time. And by ensuring that a budget addressing events, time, and money is part of every engagement letter, you significantly increase the chances of collecting your fee. Why? The client understands what to expect and agrees in advance to the process you've outlined.

A Collaborative Process

Budgeting begins by learning as much as possible about client goals and expectations. This includes getting information about parties, claims, anticipated strategies, and desired outcomes. In fact, "winning" might not be a desired outcome. A client may wish to delay the final outcome for political or financial reasons, believing that a continued threat of litigation may bring a negotiated resolution. Understanding the client's objectives is the prerequisite of the budgeting process. The key here is not just preparing the budget, but involving the client in its preparation.

Without client buy-in and approval, budgets are meaningless. The budgeting process, including all subsequent communication, must be a collaborative effort. If the client and the lawyer can't trust one another, or they take an adversarial tone, the representation will likely be unsuccessful—and collecting the fee may be more difficult. Collaboration means communication. Openness and candor right from the start will make the entire representation easier and more successful.

Signs of Trouble

In preparing the engagement letter, detailed negotiations can prevent a client from having unrealistic expectations about results *or* believing that your estimates, whether of time, outcome, or costs, are guarantees rather than informed estimates. Negotiating engagement terms will also provide a heads up on whether a client is likely to chronically complain or demand constant attention.

If at the end of the budgeting process a client asserts that you are too expensive, the logical response is to say that your other clients have found their investment in their matters has been more than justified by the results. If that response doesn't achieve the desired effect, you might suggest that the best choice for the client may be to find other counsel, because your fees are not negotiable. This is likely to produce one of two favorable results: (1) The client will be impressed with your tough negotiation skills and thus will accept your terms of engagement, or (2) the client will leave—but will spread the word that you must be highly qualified because you are aggressive, expensive, and unapologetic.

Three Key Parameters

Understanding the client's objectives is essential to defining these three key budget parameters:

1. **Time.** Use common sense, be realistic, and communicate accurately about the amount of time it will take to complete any work. Err on the side of caution and be sure to build in more than adequate time. Unless you are dealing with statutory or deal-making deadlines, clients typically are less concerned with a fast response and more concerned about unwanted surprises. Be realistic and try to build in some leeway for unforeseen difficulties.

2. **Money.** Clients should have in mind how much money they want to spend to resolve a problem, just as they know what they want to spend on a piece of equipment. In both instances, a higher initial cost may be acceptable if the long-term return on investment justifies it. Sometimes a legal problem is large enough to justify spending big sums. Resolving most issues, however, is just part of the everyday cost of doing business. It makes no sense to budget $2 million to try a case if a $100,000 settlement will meet the client's objectives.

3. **Form.** It is important to determine the format in which your client wants to receive and monitor a budget. Some clients may want an Excel

spreadsheet, while others may prefer a simple text document. A good rule of thumb is to find out how the client's own operating budget is set up and then try to integrate with it. Providing budgets and budget communication in a format that's difficult for the client to use simply defeats the collaborative nature of the process.

Subsequent Communication

After the client formally approves the budget, all subsequent communication about it must be a collaborative effort. As with the engagement agreement, have the client initial his or her approval of the budget. Because you and your client each will have unique information at any given time, you must schedule frequent communication about case developments to keep the budget on track. Review the budget document periodically, informing the client how much has already been spent and requesting approval of any necessary changes.

Failure to communicate often means failure to get paid. A large law firm once engaged me to help end its litigation fee write-offs. I suggested creating a flowchart of the litigation process to determine where and how much the firm's clients had really been involved in their cases. The resulting flowchart demonstrated that there were very few points at which the clients had been apprised of case developments. Thus, when the final bills came, they were shocked at the large amounts and refused to pay. The lawyers defended themselves by saying, "We talked with the clients frequently. We were preparing for depositions

Keeping on Track

Flowcharts are useful means for laying out case plans, developments, and budget elements. Here is a general illustration of the broad categories that might be included in a flowchart for a litigation matter. Based on the particulars of the specific case, many other additional steps and subcategories would be listed under the major plan elements below.

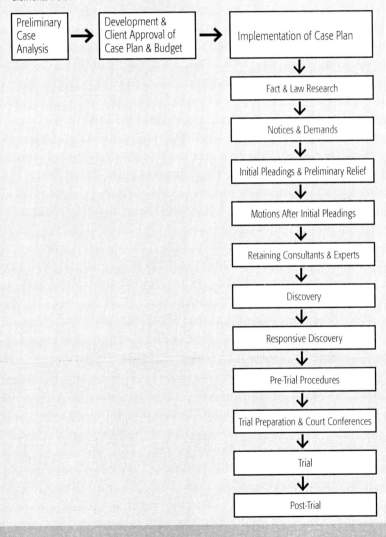

Preliminary Case Analysis → Development & Client Approval of Case Plan & Budget → Implementation of Case Plan

↓

Fact & Law Research

↓

Notices & Demands

↓

Initial Pleadings & Preliminary Relief

↓

Motions After Initial Pleadings

↓

Retaining Consultants & Experts

↓

Discovery

↓

Responsive Discovery

↓

Pre-Trial Procedures

↓

Trial Preparation & Court Conferences

↓

Trial

↓

Post-Trial

and constantly asking for documents, etc." But that's not the kind of interaction that gives clients a sense of where they are relative to their budgets.

Use of Informed Judgment

While no lawyer wants to lose control of an assignment or the direction a matter may take, making the budget a collaborative process by accepting informed client judgment can benefit both sides. To illustrate, an assistant general counsel for a major corporation told me that she once saved her company nearly half a million dollars in one litigation by working with outside counsel to develop a budget for both events and money. How did she do it?

The general counsel reduced the number of depositions outside counsel desired. In response to the law firm's concern about potential accusations of negligence or malpractice if one of the canceled depositions might prove to be a key information source, the general counsel accepted responsibility for the reduced number of depositions. She believed she was taking a reasonable business risk—something her corporate organization did every day in its sales and production departments. As a result, they reached an agreement, incurred lower costs, and achieved a successful engagement—which clearly are the objectives of any budget.

Section 4:

Client Trust Accounts

Subject to the Rules of Professional Conduct, an engagement agreement will typically control (except for unconscionable or unreasonable charges) the relationship and the payment agreement between client and lawyer. Whether fees charged and paid should be deposited into the client's trust account or the lawyer's general account is not pertinent to this discussion. Suffice it to say that payment for work performed is generally to be deposited into a general account and payment for work yet to be performed is generally to be deposited into a client's trust account.

The engagement agreement stipulates how and when the lawyer gets paid. In addition, it sets forth in detail the circumstances under which funds may or must be transferred from the client's trust account to the lawyer's general account. When the lawyer is entitled to make the transfer, the lawyer *must* make the transfer—or be guilty of commingling his or her personal funds with the client's funds—a "no-no" under the Rules of Professional Conduct.

Disciplinary Rule Requirements

The ABA Model Rules of Professional Responsibility specifically addresses the issue of trust accounts and commingling of funds. Disciplinary Rule DR 9-102, "Preserving Identity of Funds and Property of a Client," states that:

(A) All funds of clients paid to a lawyer or law firm, other than advances for costs and expenses, shall be deposited in one or more identifiable bank accounts maintained in the state in which the law office is situated and no funds belonging to the lawyer or law firm shall be deposited therein except as follows:

(1) Funds reasonably sufficient to pay bank charges may be deposited therein.

(2) Funds belonging in part to a client and in part presently or potentially to the lawyer or law firm must be deposited therein, but the portion belonging to the lawyer or law firm may be withdrawn when due unless the right of the lawyer or law firm

to receive it is disputed by the client, in which event the disputed portion shall not be withdrawn until the dispute is finally resolved.

The conclusion to be drawn from this requirement is that money earned by a lawyer for provision of services belongs to the lawyer and must be removed from the client's trust account when earned. This must be done immediately—unless jurisdictional rules state otherwise—with the earned money being placed in the lawyer's general account.

Trust versus General Accounts

When you first receive funds, you need to determine whether to deposit them into the trust account or the general account. Use this as a rule of thumb:

- ► If the funds are provided on retainer, then they are for a task that is not completed—thus, the hours are not yet earned. This means the money goes into the client trust account.

- ► If the funds have been earned when you receive them, then they should go into the general account.

Note that some jurisdictions may place additional requirements on the withdrawal of funds from a trust account. Wisconsin, for example, requires that before withdrawing any funds from the client trust account, the lawyer must give the client five days' notice. This is the case even when the funds are earned, and even if the engagement agreement provides for immediate withdrawal. It is thus important to verify the rules in your jurisdiction before making an immediate withdrawal of earned funds.

Flat, Retained, and Split Fees

If you charge a flat fee and agree that it is earned on receipt, you must withdraw the funds. It may be better to deposit the flat fee into a client's trust account and withdraw it when reaching specific events that qualify as services for which fees are earned, such as the filing of a complaint or the signing of a settlement or merger agreement.

Even retainer fees can be deposited into a general account if the agreement says that the retainer is not for future work but is instead for the lawyer specifically being engaged (and thus taken off the market). In other words, there is a valid charge for not being available to others. Opinions on the subject suggest that the retainer for this purpose must be "reasonable," again as negotiated and detailed in the engagement agreement. If you receive a retainer for future work, it would seem best to put this into your client's trust account. However, it again is best that the engagement agreement provide for this upon realizing a certain date or event.

When discussing flat or fixed fees, the hours involved are irrelevant. If you compute the flat fee based on the number of hours you anticipate and discuss that with the client (suggesting that the fee will increase if actual hours exceed the estimate), that looks like hourly billing.

Some lawyers split the fee, making part of it a nonrefundable retainer and placing the balance into the trust account for withdrawal as work is performed. This method may be preferable because it makes a clear distinction between the two elements: one nonrefundable, and one to be paid only when earned or work is performed. Even with the latter, specify the

SAMPLE CLIENT TRUST ACCOUNT SCHEDULE

(as of _____)
(month end)

	Client Name	Amount in Trust	Expected Date of Distribution	Type of Case	Comments
1		$			
2					
3					
4					
5					
6					
7					
8					
9					
10					
11					
12					
13					
14					
15					
16					
17					
18					
19					
20					
21					
22					
23					
24					
25					
TOTALS		$			

event or date that will trigger allowing you to take money from the trust account and place it into the general account. This will prevent having to wait for the client to say "yes" after the fact—and will allow you to get the money sooner.

Trust Account Access

To be certain of payment, the lawyer should include a provision in the engagement letter that the client authorizes the lawyer to debit client trust account funds after a specified time from the date of billing. This could be 15, 30, or 45 days—whichever is most reasonable under the circumstances. This provides a date certain for payment to the lawyer. In most jurisdictions, the client will retain the right to dispute the charges, though clients are unlikely to do so if they understand that, by agreement, they need to be timely with any objections. The real issue, however, is that when the fee is earned, it must be withdrawn from the client's trust account. Otherwise, it's commingling— which violates the Rules of Professional Conduct.

Commingling

Commingling is potentially a major problem. Bar associations generally have taken the attitude that even $100 of personal funds in a client's trust account is commingling of the lawyer's and client's funds. Today, most banks do not require a deposit of your own funds to open a trust account, so resist any request to do so. This may require discussion—and perhaps negotiation—with your bank. In addition, you may want to look at whether any "treaty" might exist between your state's bar and banking associations. In California, there is a treaty agreement between the two associations that permits banks to do certain things that otherwise would be considered the unauthorized practice of law, with some of the elements of the treaty applying to the management or administration of client trust accounts and escrowed funds. Be sure to check your local jurisdiction.

The engagement agreement should include a "protest process." This should provide that if you don't receive a complaint or dispute in writing from the client within the number of days set forth in your engagement agreement from the date of the invoice or statement, the client will be deemed to have approved the billing. If the client protests later, you will have a *prima facie* reason for the transfer and the money will be in your pocket (not the trust account), except as otherwise provided in your jurisdiction's rules. If your jurisdiction requires, however, you may have to transfer the disputed amount back to the trust account.

If the client protests later, you will have a *prima facie* reason for the transfer and the money will be in your pocket (not the trust account), except as otherwise provided in your jurisdiction's rules.

Tracking Problems

A particularly troublesome situation develops if lawyers are unable to track the owners of client trust account money. This can easily happen in active personal injury or debt collection law practices, or in large real estate practices. Here are some examples:

- ► Money is received in settlement of a claim and deposited into the client's trust account. Checks are then written to lien holders and mailed. Some of the lien holders fail to cash the checks, but they (not the lawyer or the client) are still entitled to the funds.

- ► A conflict arises over disbursement of trust account funds. The dispute lingers, is never resolved, and is forgotten—but the disputed funds remain in the account.

- ► Funds for a real estate deal are held back for a triggering event, such as landscaping that never happens. But no one tells the lawyer, who is waiting for disbursement instructions.

- ► A law office employee makes an erroneous or incomplete bookkeeping entry in trust account records, which is not found until long after the employee takes a new job. Now the lawyer, who did not make the entry, has funds whose owner's identity is no longer clear.

Every state imposes a fiduciary duty to properly account for client funds to prevent misappropriation (theft) or negligence. Banks are required to notify the bar association of any such defalcations, and a bounced check from a client trust account brings the bar into the lawyer's office almost immediately. But what if a problem inadvertently occurs but the bar doesn't know about the surplus? One expensive resolution is to hire an outside accountant to go through every document, check, and ledger to reconcile the account. Another suggestion is to open and operate through a new trust account with scrupulously "clean" records, while allowing the old account to sift through until only the few questionable items remain. At least then, so the theory goes, you will have only a small problem.

Such alternatives miss the point, however. The lawyer is a fiduciary who must keep accurate accounting records under the state's rules. This may require having an outside accountant reconcile trust and bank account records each month. It should also involve the law office diligently maintaining the necessary information by using a reliable software program such as QuickBooks or the like. To do less is to invite inquiry—and trouble.

Section 5:

Pricing Services by Value Billing

Several years ago a national law firm drew considerable attention with an ad campaign that challenged the billable hour. Many firms use billing alternatives, but this firm distinguished itself simply by raising the taboo topic of billing ethics. "The longer lawyers take, the more they make," one ad said. "Does that align their interest with yours?"

Apply that question to a taxi driver in New York, where the rules for taxi use allow cabs to be shared. Let's assume one person engages a taxi at a fee of $30 while a second person engaging the same taxi is told that the fee is $20. On the face of it, this is double billing. The taxi company is now getting $50 from two passengers sharing the cab, when it would only get $30 for a single-passenger cab ride. Is there anything unethical about this? Not at all. Taxi companies charge a fixed fee based on the value of the ride, not based on the time. (Time may be an element of the costing equation that enables a profit calculation, but it is not a pricing component.)

Contrast this with the ethical dilemma of lawyers, the majority of whom bill based on time alone. If a lawyer is sitting on a plane or waiting at a courthouse to handle a matter for Client A, can he or she use that time to do work for Client B? Most states' Rules of Professional Conduct require billing only one client at a time because billable minutes are the measure of the fee.

But lawyers that do not bill based on time can increase their profit (sometimes called take-home pay) when they become more efficient in providing their services or products. Lawyers don't really sell time; we sell a service. Our goal should be to provide value—advice that translates into solutions for our clients. Hourly billing doesn't address value and benefits—the service's worth, as opposed to its cost.

Increasing Perceptions of Value

"Good service," "value," and "solutions" shouldn't be vague buzzwords. All lawyers—whether they are solo practitioners or members of megafirms—can structure their services to consistently foster a perception of high value for their clients. Here are basic elements of how to do so:

- ▶ Establish a return phone call policy. Return or have an assistant return client phone calls within two to four hours.

- ▶ Know your clients' concerns and understand their business.

- ▶ Create a client-friendly office environment. Have informative literature in the waiting room and make sure it's available in your clients' primary languages.

- ▶ Prepare your clients for interactive events such as negotiation sessions, depositions, and testimony so they know what to expect. Incorporate a wide range of possibilities so that clients are not shocked if the outcome, over which you have no control, is different from what they had hoped.

- ▶ Never make promises you can't keep.

- ▶ Regularly ask clients for feedback about whether they are pleased with your services. This feedback should be focused on their satisfaction with the service provided rather than on the results achieved.

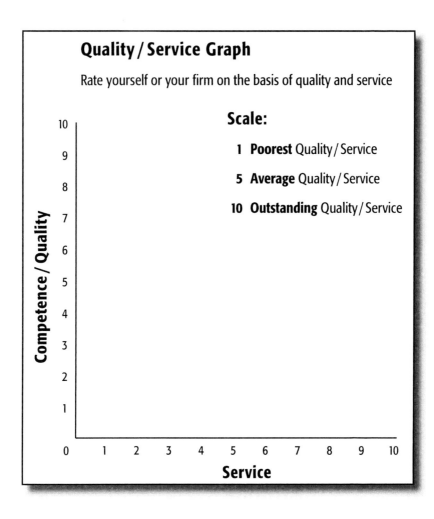

Quality / Service Graph

Rate yourself or your firm on the basis of quality and service

Scale:

1 Poorest Quality / Service

5 Average Quality / Service

10 Outstanding Quality / Service

Competence / Quality (vertical axis): 1, 2, 3, 4, 5, 6, 7, 8, 9, 10

Service (horizontal axis): 0, 1, 2, 3, 4, 5, 6, 7, 8, 9, 10

Another way to define and provide value is to establish what marketers call a unique selling proposition. Be different. Offer something that your competitors don't or can't provide. Create something new that your clients need or want. If you can't think of what makes you unique, you're really nothing more than a commodity to your clients.

A unique selling proposition is a key strategy in establishing higher rates. It can be approached in a variety of ways.

If you handle estate planning, for example, you could add financial planning as a service, either as part of the fee package or for a designated added fee. Or, sometimes showing that you provide better-than-excellent service is all you need to establish a unique position. For instance, you can show that you use state-of-the-art technology tools to better serve clients and their needs. Having an effective electronic knowledge management program with a shared database that makes comprehensive information available faster and more completely to clients and others in the firm is one way to demonstrate your technological edge. The result is greater efficiency, better communication, and faster turnaround. All of these can justify a higher effective hourly rate.

Charging for Ancillary Services

The Rules of Professional Conduct, of course, require that charges be "reasonable." There is a great deal of latitude here, especially in terms of customary practices by lawyers in your community. Legitimate charges are not unprofessional. You've done the work and should be paid for it.

The starting point for any charge is the fee provisions contained in the engagement agreement. Document everything for which you expect payment at the stated rate. Consider including the following items.

Another way to define and provide value is to establish what marketers call a unique selling proposition. Be different. Offer something that your competitors don't or can't provide.

Client communication. This should include electronic communications, as well as traditional letters and telephone calls. Given the informality of e-mail, few lawyers truly capture the time they spend on this legitimate form of client communication. Like phone conversation, e-mail communication concerning client matters represents billable time. Yet in their rapid-fire multitasking, lawyers often don't note their time when sending e-mails. And if they don't do it then, by the end of the day—let alone by the end of the week—they will forget how much time was involved. As a result, they may end up with incomplete billing, frequently resulting in 15 to 20 percent less revenue for the lawyer.

Ancillary charges. Some lawyers charge their clients for "opening" a file on each matter; others charge for photocopying the file before giving it to the client when requested. These are legitimate charges to clients if specified in the retainer agreement. The fact that the client owns his or her own file does not prohibit the lawyer from contracting to copy it at the client's expense. Of course, if your competitors do not make such charges or if your client feels "nickel and dimed" for them, charging may not be worthwhile. In the final analysis, costs should be viewed not as a profit center, but instead as overhead covered by your fee.

Administrative activity. Filing a notice of unavailability or a notice of continuance before an extended absence from the office is often in the client's best interest and can be considered billable. Indeed, one can argue that failure to file such notices is a failure to protect the client. If opposing counsel doesn't know you will be on vacation and files a motion or other action requiring a special appearance or a later motion of continuance, the client will ultimately pay more than he or she would have paid for a simple notice.

Even if you decide against charging for a particular action, at least show the time spent, the normal charge, and a courtesy discount. It may educate your client—and be a useful bit of marketing.

Justifying a Fee Increase

The positive side of the pricing equation is that demonstrating your value enables you to make a convincing case for raising your fees. This is always tricky, though, and generally hinges on two factors:

- ▶ **Qualitative considerations.** These generally involve ethical questions of professional conduct. Is the fee reasonable and in proportion to the value of the services performed? Does the lawyer have the skill and experience to justify the fee? Does the client understand the amount and nature of the fee and consent to it? Answering no to any of these questions means a fee increase is not warranted.

- ▸ **Quantitative considerations.** These typically reduce to market factors. Your new fee must be competitive with others in your geographic and practice areas. You must know the current market conditions and the competitive pressures on legal fees. Each local market has its own characteristics. National trends are interesting but don't control your situation.

Assuming you pass the qualitative and quantitative tests, the question then becomes how best to make the case for raising your fees. The lawyer who thinks in terms of value can make one or more of these five arguments:

1. **You add value.** In other words, what you add in terms of service costs less than the increase. For example, in any type of practice, providing faster turnaround from engagement to completion is a key way of adding value.

2. **You achieve results.** If you raise fees going forward after clients are happy because you've won a motion or negotiated a favorable deal—even if somewhat before or beyond your normal billing date—the fees are more likely to be accepted. This places the client on the peak of the "satisfaction curve"—the time of least resistance for accepting an increase. Do it later and the client will invariably forget how important you were in achieving the result and may resist.

3. **You are reasonable.** All other things being equal, the smaller the fee increase, the easier it is for clients to accept it. Adding 3 to 5 percent to an hourly fee won't turn off many clients. Remember, for the average client, there is little price sensitivity in choosing a lawyer. More than 60 percent of lawyer-client relationships come about because of referrals from trusted friends or reputed legal ability. In these instances, clients generally are willing to understand and accept modest fee increases.

4. **You handle a big-ticket or break-the-company case.** In these instances, price typically doesn't seem to matter. The client's options are limited and the perception of need—and therefore value—is high. When matters are serious and precedent setting, clients simply want whomever they perceive to be the best.

5. **You are cutting-edge.** Clients don't want their lawyer to reinvent the wheel. For example, once you've done the research or created the template, electronic knowledge management through a shared database makes detailed information available faster and more completely to clients and others in the firm. In other words, clients will pay for the research once, not multiple times, and they can now expect your firm to use the same research in similar future matters without paying a new fee for the same research or document template each time it is used. That added value can justify a higher effective hourly

rate, especially for corporate clients who reward continuous improvement.

There is no perfect time to raise fees. Those clients who do not want to pay a higher fee will seek other counsel. Those who believe your service to be of value will accept the higher fee and remain with you. It's a simple equation—provided that value is on your side.

Unbundling Services

Of course, even for lawyers who consistently provide and document value, there are times when price concerns can lead clients, particularly corporate ones, to request lower billing rates. Value billing does not entirely alleviate client pressure concerning fees. But the advantage of charging for value is that rather than lowering one's rate, the lawyer is in a position to take a certain value or given service off the table to deliver a lower price to the client. In effect, when the client wants a reduced price, you can "unbundle" services to accomplish that objective—meaning you charge a different price for a different group of tasks or functions.

For example, consider the components of an hourly fee. If returned phone calls within two hours are part of your regular hourly rate, take that response time off the table if you lower your hourly rate in response to the client's request. Tell the client that your response time will be up to 48 hours. The point will be clear: You are not lowering your price, you are simply adjusting the value composition to reflect what the client is buying.

Or, say that the matter involves litigation and you agree with the client that you will perform particular services on a discrete basis, as opposed to handling all aspects of the litigation. For example, you could agree with the client that you will handle only the drafting of initial pleadings and make an appearance at an order-to-show-cause hearing, and that other elements are to be handled personally by the client or by a third-party chosen by, or at the behest of, the client.

This way, the client gets the message that you're modifying the price to fit the appropriate level based on the services to be delivered. In other words, for x dollars you will do "this" and for y dollars, you will do "this" less "ABC." While "ABC" may not be of particular importance in resolving the client's matter, the client gets the message that you are adjusting the price to fit the appropriate level based on the services to be delivered.

Communicating Value

Regardless of your specific billing approach, ultimately you enable clients to judge your value by how much you interact with them. You need to take a customer-service approach to dealing with clients, just as your favorite shops or restaurants do with you. Even the simplest steps to accomplish this can pay big dividends. Here are some examples:

- ► Make sure staff members know the names of your clients. Give everyone the client list so that they never have to ask the spelling of a name when taking a message or appointment.

- Make your clients feel like part of the team. Seek out their opinions and ask them what they want to accomplish. Explain the reasons behind your advice.

- Visit clients at their homes or businesses. You'll get a better understanding of what is important to them, and they'll develop greater trust in you. Don't charge for the visit—but be sure it shows up on your next statement as a "no charge" item.

- Solicit client feedback. This doesn't require an elaborate questionnaire. Simply meet clients over coffee and ask, "How am I doing? Should I be doing something differently? Is there an issue that concerns you? Does my staff treat you courteously?" Given this opportunity, clients will provide you with honest answers. And if there's a problem, it's better to know now rather than later when there's an unpaid bill or a disciplinary charge against you.

In short, communicate regularly with clients. Don't wait for them to come to you. Return their calls promptly. Send them copies of all relevant documents that come in or are sent out from the office. Provide status reports on a regular basis. Demonstrating the work you do is the best way to ensure getting paid.

Section 6:

Alternative Pricing Methods

Deciding to reject hourly rates is not the same as knowing how to replace them with a better billing method. Clients want change, yes, but most are unable to truly initiate it themselves. The closest most clients come is the request for proposal (RFP) "beauty contest," which often has a checklist of specific items that supposedly will be evaluated on a weighted basis—but which frequently comes down to which RFP respondent offers the lowest hourly rate. Most clients recognize the importance of and are willing to pay a fair fee for value. What they do not want is to pay too much, or to pay for inefficiencies, duplications, or unnecessary services. This is the starting point for other billing alternatives that incorporate the value billing concept but are more structured in approach.

Making Alternatives Work: The Foundation

Full-scale commitment to using alternative billing requires commitment to these three basic premises for success:

1. **Communication is essential.** Surveys uniformly show that clients are unhappier with surprises and unexplained costs in their bills than they are with high bills. No firm should fall into the trap of simply cutting fees because it sends a message that the firm was overcharging in the first place. An up-front general statement about fees and alternatives, estimates and budgets, and flowcharts to explain who in the firm does what are all crucial communication tools. It is important to tailor these communications, and the fees themselves, to individual client preferences—which, after all, define the perception of value.

2. **Clients, including corporate counsel, are not particularly knowledgeable about billing.** Law firms must seize the initiative by working with clients to develop specific pricing alternatives based on

each client's preferences. Being proactive avoids having the client fixate on fee alternatives that may be unworkable.

3. **There is no universal best billing alternative.** Client preferences and each firm's operations differ, and each project or case has a multitude of factors that could accommodate various billing options.

Primary Methods

With the forgoing premises accepted and the needed commitments made, the question becomes which billing alternatives to use. There is nothing magical about hourly rate alternatives—they all seek to achieve the same thing. The goal is to deliver value as perceived by the client for a total price deemed to be appropriate and reasonable by both client and attorney. Choosing the right alternative is ultimately a business matter for both the firm and the client. Alternative approaches can include any of the following.

Blended hourly rate. The client is charged one fee per hour regardless of who in the firm works on the matter—be it a senior partner with a high rate or a junior lawyer with a lower rate. The right balance gives clients a better price, and it gives firms the financial incentive to delegate work.

Fixed or flat fee. The fee is determined and stipulated in the engagement letter, before the assignment even begins. It will not vary regardless of how much time the lawyer expends, or what the result is. Flat fees are especially useful for routine legal services.

Contingent or percentage fee. Frequently used in personal injury and collection matters, this fee constitutes a percentage of the value recovered for the client. This approach may also be used in certain defense matters.

Premium pricing. An hourly rate or some other billing method is used as the base, and the lawyer is able to add on an additional premium if the result exceeds client expectations. Of course, there is no premium if the outcome is not successful. Premium pricing gives the lawyer a stake in the outcome and the assurance of a minimum fee even for a "bad" result.

Retainer. This method sets up a fixed fee for a fixed time cycle (often monthly) during a designated period (often one year). The "true retainer" is typically used as a one-time payment to guarantee the availability of the lawyer or firm at a future date. A retainer may also be used, for example, when the client has an uncertain number of matters and both the lawyer and the client agree that matters of a certain nature (e.g., product liability claims) in a certain geographic area (e.g., Southern California) will be handled by the lawyer in exchange for a designated sum (e.g., $25,000 per month through the term of the retainer agreement, such as one year).

Value billing. Rather than setting price by a standard unit or result, value billing lists actions taken to benefit the client. Personalized service, rapid return of calls and e-mails, unexpectedly good results—these

There is nothing magical about hourly rate alternatives—
they all seek to achieve the same thing. The goal is to
deliver value as perceived by the client for a total price
deemed to be appropriate and reasonable by both client
and attorney.

are all examples of value-added actions that the lawyer
can demonstrate and charge for, or for which the
client can pay a bonus.

Combining Options

Most firms use an analysis to determine the mix of
hourly rates that should be used to accomplish the
work for given matters. However, almost any case or
project can be broken into tasks, and each task can
be priced separately and differently to create multiple
pricing schemes within a single transaction based on
client preferences and value perceptions. Different
clients can be approached differently. Creating a
matrix can demonstrate to clients those areas where
costs can be controlled and can also educate clients
about what can be done to lower the overall cost of a
project.

Following is one example of such a matrix applied to
an acquisition transaction. It shows various steps in
the process, and whether they could be billed at the

hourly rate of each attorney, a blend or average of all hourly rates, a fixed price, or a percentage of the transaction value. The purpose of this table is not to suggest that all the pricing options should be used on each task; rather, it indicates that it is perfectly legitimate for the firm to pick and choose which pricing option is most effective and appropriate at any given stage in the transaction. The choice should, of course, be made very clear to the client in the final billing.

Tasks in the Transaction	Pricing Options for Each Task			
	Hourly	Blended Hourly	Fixed Cost	Agreed Percent Option
Letter of intent	X		X	
Draft preliminary purchase and sale agreement	X		X	
Negotiations	X			X
Final draft agreement and site agreements	X	X		
Due diligence	X	X	X	X
Closing	X			
Post-closing agenda	X	X	X	
X = possible pricing options				

While opinions vary on which alternative provides the best measure of value to a client, the fixed fee is the most frequently used alternative billing method. Fixed fees can include retainers, task-based flat rates, or contingent or percentage fees. The latter variant, the contingency fee, is the second most frequently used alternative billing method, although it mainly applies to litigation. Note that public policy prevents use of contingency or percentage fees in some matters such as criminal defense or dissolution of marriage. Because the fixed fee and the contingency fee are both so popular, we will consider them at greater length in the next section of this report.

Maintaining Control

The best alternative billing methods reflect a highly interactive process: The lawyer takes a direct financial stake in achieving the desired results, and the client plays an active role in deciding whether those results have been met. No lawyer wants to lose control and direction of an assignment, but absorbing a degree of risk and accepting informed client judgment are often essential elements of a strong and growing lawyer-client relationship.

There are firms that have affirmatively embraced this changed dynamic. Chicago's Ungaretti & Harris has for a decade offered "guaranteed" satisfaction to its clients. Here is the firm's definition of this concept: "We guarantee that as our client you will receive cost-effective legal services delivered in a timely manner. We promise to involve you and communicate with you regularly. We cannot guarantee outcomes; we do guarantee your satisfaction with our service. If we do not perform to your satisfaction, inform us promptly. We will resolve the issue to your satisfaction, even if it means reducing your legal fees."

A guarantee of value can be either general or specific. There can, of course, be no guarantee of results; but the firm can guarantee that it will work with the client to ensure that the client's perception of value has been met. Ultimately there is no way to make a guarantee risk-free. However, the upside potential is great. Guarantees cut through the clutter in the marketplace and identify a firm as being committed to value, rather than just making claims and assertions.

Section 7:

Fixed or Flat Fees: Further Exploration

As noted in Section 6, fixed fees are the most popular alternative to hourly billing. From the client's point of view, the fixed fee enables advance planning for the charges to be made. For the lawyer, the fixed fee provides the opportunity to charge for value, not for hours spent. With a fixed or flat fee, the billing rate is determined at the matter's start and stipulated in the engagement letter. It will not vary no matter how much time the lawyer expends or what the ultimate result is.

Flat fees are especially useful for routine legal services, and they also encourage the use of technology to streamline the provision of those services. At its most extreme, this is embodied in "do-it-yourself" Web sites purporting to charge a fixed fee for advice, research, and forms in such areas as family law, probate, real estate closings, and even patent filings. But there are other, more sophisticated examples of the same concept. General Electric, for example, has created a "tool kit" of clauses available on its secure intranet for use by its sales force to change terms and words of standard contracts when customers request. In such instances, the GE sales force used to send the contract back to GE lawyers for review and change, a costly and time-consuming process. Now, providing standard term alternatives online saves GE and its clients a substantial amount of time and, therefore, legal fees.

Let's consider the central issues involved in the fixed fee process for law firms.

Determining the Fixed Rate

A flat fee system can only work where there is precise knowledge about the scope of services to be provided and the cost of those services (not necessarily equated to the price charged). Or, put differently, a flat fee is only an acceptable billing alternative if the lawyer knows the cost structure behind it and if the client accepts the value that the fee represents.

Unfortunately, lawyers generally don't know their costs of operation. Thus, the fee figure often is chosen "by guess, by golly," not based on a cost-benefit analysis. Beware: Your firm cannot aspire to set an accurate flat fee unless you understand the operation of the firm as a business (budget, collections, profit, loss, etc.), the firm's billing structure, and how each attorney determines firm profitability.

Beware: Your firm cannot aspire to set an accurate flat fee unless you understand the operation of the firm as a business, the firm's billing structure, and how each attorney determines firm profitability.

Consider the example of a contract attorney doing work for a large law firm. The firm proposed a new, higher fee schedule that included a volume discount based on a scaled number of hours per month. The law firm's managing partner asked that the number of hours and the discount to be applied be reviewed retroactively at the end of each three months' cycle. But a volume discount at a flat fee should be based on a prospective, rather than a retrospective, guarantee of work. A retrospective review is a disaster for the lawyer because it fails to offer any security and makes planning impossible. Without the prospective assurance of volume, there is little or no benefit to the contract lawyer; there is every benefit to the client law firm. This is analogous to the philosophy that an option-holder is the beneficiary of an option. In this example, a prospective arrangement gives the "option" to the contract lawyer; a retrospective arrangement gives the "option" to the contracting law firm.

Negotiating the Rate

Flat fees are often considered to be a form of discount. Lawyers endanger their interests by accepting discounts on their rates and should approach this issue with great care.

Take as another example an intellectual property lawyer who is approached by a prospective client with the possibility of work in return for a discounted rate for a fixed volume of work. To avoid setting a troubling precedent for rate cutting, the lawyer should consider three alternatives that meet the client's request but protect the lawyer's interests:

- ▸ First, state that your billing rate is $295. You do not talk about discounts, a reduction in fee, or any other modification of your hourly rate. To do so would be to negotiate against yourself and against your self-interest. If, in the same breath, you quote your fee and then start talking about discounts, you are saying that you are not serious about your fee.

- ▸ Second, if the client asks whether $295 is the least expensive rate you can charge, raise the idea of a volume discount. Explain that you are prepared to discount your rate from $295 to, for example, $270 but if, and only if, the client is prepared to guarantee 20 hours of work per month for a minimum period of time, say six or nine months.

- ▸ Third, if the client will commit to the amount of hours and the time period, the client should pay the discounted fee of $5,400 (20 hours at $270 per hour) at the beginning of each month. In other words, the client has to prepay that amount. Then if the client needs more than 20 hours of work in any given month, the additional work will be billed at the discounted $270 rate under billing terms the attorney typically uses (for example, payable within 30 days of the billing).

Approaching the idea of discounting in this way says that you are willing to treat clients fairly when they treat you well. In other words, the quid pro quo for a discount is a guarantee with payment up front. It makes no sense to do business with a client who will not agree to do that.

The Contingency Fee Alternative

Another aspect of the fixed fees discussion worth considering involves a flat fee rate that pays the lawyer a premium for success. In particular, we are talking here about contingency fee arrangements. Such arrangements can include full contingency fees; partial contingency fees (i.e., the lawyer receives a discounted hourly rate while the matter is pending, plus the contingency percentage of amount won or recovered); reverse contingency fees in defense work (i.e., the client and the lawyer agree in advance on the value of the judgment sought, and the lawyer gets a percentage of the difference if the award is below the target); and refundable retainers in which any unused portion is returned to the client.

Frequently used in personal injury and collection matters, a contingency fee is a flat percentage of the value recovered for the client. It is particularly useful for the lawyer skilled at analyzing cases and accepting those with a high likelihood of success. However, it is also becoming an accepted alternative to give corporate firms a bigger payoff on bet-the-company matters for large clients, and to give those clients the assurance that their lawyer has some "skin in the game" in exchange for the predetermined percentage payout. Sounds intriguing but, as was noted in *The Wall Street Journal* article "Knives Out? Law Firms in New Era" by Nathan Koppel (March 7, 2007), corporate law firms that enter into contingency arrangements face increased problems from their use—particularly if the firm wins the matter. One such challenge is justifying a very large fee resulting from a very large judgment or settlement. This is generally a matter of public outrage or amazement, caused by a lack of appreciation for the generally large investment of time and expert fees expended by the law firm—and, of course, the high probability of risk of defeat when the law firm first agreed to represent this client or class of client.

Some of these problems from the lawyer side crop up while the contingency matter is open. Normally, compensation is based on hours worked and dollars collected. So how can you compensate lawyers who bring no money into the firm, and, in fact, are responsible for many dollars "flowing out of the firm" in the form of their compensation and expenses advanced to sustain the lawsuit? How can the firm determine appropriate bonuses? When millions of dollars are involved, the tension can become palpable.

Then, when the firm is successful and many dollars flow into the law firm, who gets what? How much should the lawyers working on the matter receive? What kind of bonus should they receive, if any? Isn't the matter the "property" of the firm? Didn't the firm, not the lawyers, advance the costs? What is fair? What will keep all the lawyers happy and in place? What will reduce the urge to leave and go to another law firm? And what should departed lawyers who worked on the contingency matters receive? A belated bonus or a payoff upon their departure? How would you value the matter, before knowing even if the firm won the case?

These questions really have only one good answer. As long as any firm follows the "eat what you kill" compensation model, in which all attorneys are rewarded based on how much business they personally bring in, contingency fees will cause problems. Any firm that encourages lawyers to maximize their individual compensation may have fast near-term growth. But approaching compensation as an institution makes for greater firm harmony and longevity. It also is the best foundation for nonhourly billing alternatives.

If a firm wants to promote cooperative effort that ensures its survival, it must change to a more cooperative compensation model that depends on the success of the organization. That way the burdens and rewards of contingency billing are shared equally, and the firm benefits along with its clients.

Section 8:

Refunded Fees and Fees Not Yet Earned

EARNED VS UNEARNED

Charging a flat fee can raise a related issue of whether that fee can—or should—be refundable. Consider the example of a lawyer who has an estate planning practice and provides for flat fees that are nonrefundable. In one instance, a client requested an estate plan. The lawyer completed the documents and sent them to the client for signature. The client then informed the lawyer that she had changed her mind and did not want the type of trust that the lawyer had created. Worse, at this point she wanted the fee refunded. As a matter of professional courtesy, the lawyer made an adjustment that the client accepted. But months later, the same client filed a complaint with bar counsel. Bar counsel then called this lawyer to challenge the lawyer's fee structure. Bar counsel went further to suggest that maintaining a record of hours billed is a requirement.

Refundable Fee Issues

This case raises several issues. The first is that, according to the Rules of Professional Conduct, fees must be "reasonable." Each jurisdiction has its own standards that define this term, but the important point is that you must be able to defend the fee and the fee structure. Using an hourly standard is only one method of doing so. No jurisdiction requires that fees be charged by the hour or that a record of hours be maintained. If a flat fee meets the standard of being "reasonable," and the client knowingly accepts the fee in a written fee agreement, the lawyer charging it is within the rules.

A second issue involves whether or not value billing may be contrary to the best interests of the client because it involves no set, defined standard. Contingency lawyers are the classic examples of the use of value billing. If a client doesn't receive value (normally defined as a money award), there is no charge. If the client does receive value, the lawyer's fee is based on a previously negotiated percentage. Having said this, however, the lawyer must still show that the fee is reasonable. Bar counsel needs to protect the public in these matters and lawyers cannot be greedy.

The duty to charge a reasonable fee is not altered by credit card use.

Whether the lawyer exceeds the standard is a matter of individual review.

Special Note: While time records may not be required in either fixed fee or contingency matters, a fee dispute as to the reasonableness of a fee is often resolved by reference to time records. A lawyer's fee is voidable, or if there is a fee dispute and the lawyer is awarded *quantum meruit* (Q.M.) and the Q.M. is based on time, then there seems to be little incentive to move away from the billable hour standard.

There is a third consideration. If you take a retainer in advance, whether the fee is called "refundable" or not, and work is promised in exchange for that fee, then failure to perform the work requires a refund. It doesn't matter what you called the fee. There is some dispute concerning taking an advance fee and calling it nonrefundable, when you mean it is a minimum fee. If you do not "use up" the full advance, some would argue that you still "earned" it because it is a minimum fee. Others would argue that you are obligated to refund the difference. The former position permits deposit to the general account; the latter position requires deposit to the client's trust account.

However, if you take a fee in exchange for "coming off the market," this fee may not be refundable because you've already done the work. In other words, there is a value that can be assigned to being prevented by the rules of conflict of interest from representing the other party. Again, the rule of reasonableness comes into play.

Payment of Fees Not Yet Earned

The earlier discussion about whether credit cards can be used for payment (see Section 2, "The Engagement Letter") raises the issue of payment for legal fees not yet earned. Client payments by credit card should be only for legal services rendered—not for unearned retainers or charge-backs of unearned fees.

But in the often trend-setting state of California, the Standing Committee on Professional Responsibility and Conduct has issued Formal Opinion No. 2007-172 concerning use of credit cards for payment of earned and unearned legal fees and costs. In effect, the Committee opined that it is acceptable to use credit cards for payment of both fees earned and not yet earned, but not for costs or expenses. In the California report, the Committee cites Massachusetts Bar Association Ethics Opinion 78-11 (1978). Under that 1978 opinion, lawyers in Massachusetts may accept credit cards for both earned and unearned fees. And nearly 20 years later the Massachusetts Bar affirmed its position in Opinion 95-11, which held that an attorney may not enter into a fee agreement that requires the client to pay a nonrefundable retainer. If you take a retainer in advance—whether the fee be called "refundable" or not—and work is

From The State Bar of California Standing Committee on Professional Responsibility and Conduct Formal Opinion No. 2007-172

Issues:

1. May an attorney ethically accept payment of earned fees from a client by credit card?

2. May an attorney ethically accept payment of fees not yet earned from a client by credit card?

3. May an attorney ethically accept payment of advances for costs and expenses from a client by credit card?

Digest:

1. An attorney may ethically accept payment of earned fees from a client by credit card. In doing so, however, the attorney must discharge his or her duty of confidentiality.

2. Likewise, an attorney may ethically accept a deposit for fees not yet earned from a client by credit card, but must discharge his or her duty of confidentiality.

3. By contrast, an attorney may not ethically accept a deposit for advances for costs and expenses from a client by credit card because the attorney must deposit such advances into a client trust account and cannot do so initially because they are paid through an account that is subject to invasion.

Source: State Bar of California Web Site, http://calbar.ca.gov/calbar/ pdfs/ethics/2007-172.pdf

promised in exchange for that fee, then failure to perform the work requires a refund.

To focus on earned fees, the California opinion suggests that payment by credit card offers "parity" to both cash and check. This seems sensible, if confidentiality requirements are observed. The lawyer must describe the nature of the services to the credit card company in very general terms, such as "for professional services rendered," while of course providing a more detailed service summary to the client.

The duty to charge a reasonable fee is not altered by credit card use. And there is no fee splitting or fee sharing merely through the debit of a service charge; this is simply for the convenience of receiving payment of fees owed the attorney. Further, the attorney would normally pay these credit card service charges. Any interest or late fees the client owes are a matter for the client, not the attorney. The theory that a credit card company is an independent intermediary that can interfere with the use of the funds defies today's commercial logic. The credit card company is an implied agent-in-fact, if not one in law, of either or both the client and the lawyer. Thus, credit cards should have parity with checks and cash.

However, I do believe the California opinion strays when holding that payment of unearned fees also may be made by credit card. Contrary to most states, California does not obligate lawyers to place unearned fees into a client trust account. But for this quirk, the opinion continued, credit card payments for unearned fees would not be acceptable. Thus, this remains the best policy to follow.

Section 9:

Special Appearances

Both large and small law practices hire contract lawyers to provide legal counsel on matters for which the outsourcing attorney is unavailable. In a contract lawyer situation, the outsourcing attorney needs to oversee the outsourced legal work and communicate with the client concerning the firm-contract lawyer relationship. Contract lawyers can contribute to work and cost efficiencies if used correctly. They can also be a transparent resource (thanks to online technology) that offers a win-win solution for firms and clients.

Financial Liability for Malpractice

Attorneys in small communities—and even in major metropolitan areas—routinely make special court appearances for other lawyers as a professional courtesy, to help out with a schedule conflict or to handle a routine matter. But there are potential problems when a contract attorney makes an appearance on behalf of another lawyer. The lawyer who engages the contract "pinch hitter" obviously becomes responsible—in a malpractice sense—for any errors committed, even in a seemingly simple case.

Problems can also arise in the reverse situation, when an attorney making a special appearance becomes liable for the errors of the primary lawyer—or even of other lawyers who made previous special appearances. In the 2000 case *Streit v. Covington & Crowe*, the California Court of Appeals upheld a plaintiff's right to include the Covington & Crowe firm in a malpractice action against her own attorney. The court found an implied attorney-client relationship, even though the Covington firm's only contact with the plaintiff was an appearance made as a professional courtesy at a hearing on a summary judgment motion.

In 2003 California attempted to address this issue by creating a new "Notice of Limited Scope Representation" form that clearly delineates the

> The lawyer who engages the contract "pinch hitter" obviously becomes responsible—in a malpractice sense—for any errors committed.

purpose and duration of the special appearance and must be signed by the client, who acknowledges the special appearance's limitations by signing the form. However, notice of the special appearance must be filed with all parties of record, and any of them can file an objection with the court, which must then rule on the special appearance's acceptability. Because of these complexities, lawyers need to consider carefully whether to accept a contract assignment, especially since the court is unlikely to order payment of legal fees for this process beyond what the client agreed to pay for the initial appearance or work.

Another example of possible malpractice danger arises from the Florida Supreme Court decision in *Cowan Liebowitz & Latman, PC, et al. v. Donald Kaplan*. The court ruled that a third party who had not retained a lawyer's or law firm's services could allege legal malpractice against that lawyer or law firm. A third party who relied on a lawyer's professional services—even if rendered on behalf of another—can sue if the lawyer failed to exercise due diligence and proper care and thereby damaged the third party. The court decision permitted creditors of an insolvent corporation to sue the lawyers who

California's three-page Notice Of Limited Scope Representation Form was adopted for mandatory use by the Judicial Council of California, with the January 1, 2007, version available at www.courtinfo.ca.gov/ forms/documents/mc950.pdf. Below is page one of three.

MC-950

ATTORNEY *(Name, State Bar number, and address)*:	FOR COURT USE ONLY

TELEPHONE NO.:   FAX NO.:
E-MAIL ADDRESS:
ATTORNEY FOR *(Name)*:

SUPERIOR COURT OF CALIFORNIA, COUNTY OF
STREET ADDRESS:
MAILING ADDRESS:
CITY AND ZIP CODE:
BRANCH NAME:

PLAINTIFF/PETITIONER: CASE NUMBER:

DEFENDANT/RESPONDENT:

OTHER:

NOTICE OF LIMITED SCOPE REPRESENTATION
☐ Amended

JUDGE:
DEPT.:

[Note: This form is for use in civil cases other than family law. For family law cases, use form FL-950.]

1. Attorney *(name)*:
   and party *(name)*:
   who is the ☐ petitioner/plaintiff ☐ respondent/defendant ☐ other *(describe)*:

   have an agreement that the attorney will provide limited scope representation in this case to the party.

2. The attorney will represent the party
   a. ☐ at the hearing on *(date)*:
      ☐ and at any continuance of that hearing
      ☐ until submission of the order after hearing

   b. ☐ at the trial on *(date)*:
      ☐ and at any continuance of that trial
      ☐ until judgment

   c. ☐ other *(specify nature and duration of representation)*:

3. By signing this form, the party agrees to sign *Substitution of Attorney—Civil* (form MC-050) at the completion of the representation described above.

Form Adopted for Mandatory Use
Judicial Council of California
MC-950 [New January 1, 2007]

NOTICE OF LIMITED SCOPE REPRESENTATION

Cal. Rules of Court, rule 3.36
www.courtinfo.ca.gov

American LegalNet, Inc.
www.FormsWorkflow.com

represented the corporation, accusing them of failing to disclose material information in private placement memoranda for the sale of shares.

Fee Splitting

The issue of fees can create another potential pitfall. When firms outsource for a special appearance or other contract assignment, they are not required to bill the client at their cost for the contract attorney's time. In fact, Model Rule 1.5 holds that fee splitting is acceptable if both lawyers involved contribute something of value, if the client agrees in writing, and if the total fee is reasonable. However, it's vital that the attorneys involved have their own fee arrangement in writing. Courts from California to Michigan have ruled that split fees cannot be collected in full without complete documentation from either the client or the attorney side.

Attorneys who don't get written confirmation when they accept an outsourced contract assignment or special appearance are like the cobbler's children who go without shoes. Clearly, they have failed to take care of themselves if their only recourse to secure an undocumented special appearance fee is to sue. And when money is involved, even lawyers can have selective memories.

This discussion is distinct from the situation where a firm directly engages a contract lawyer for certain work that is paid at an hourly rate lower than the firm's standard rate for its other lawyers. In this situation, the contract lawyer is equivalent to a firm member and his or her work is billed at the firm rate. This is not deemed a cost item merely to be passed on to the client. Neither must there be a direct fee agreement with the client in this instance.

Contract arrangements can aid work and cost efficiencies if used correctly as a transparent resource. But that transparency must still include proper oversight and quality control. Court decisions make clear in different contexts that the provision of outside legal help should never be undertaken cavalierly. The financially favorable incentives may be offset by a big malpractice judgment or litigation over the fee-splitting arrangement.

Court-Ordered Fees*

A related and more specialized fee concern has to do with court-ordered fees. Both state legal codes and the U.S. Code frequently reference such court-ordered, court-approved fees for counsel employed in probate proceedings, bankruptcy proceedings, and worker's compensation proceedings, to name a few. In each of these situations, the court of original jurisdiction retains sole authority to determine the propriety of legal fees arising out of the underlying legal action.

In some situations, however, while contribution for attorney's fees (and costs) is ordered as part of a civil proceeding, the fees are not set by statute. For example, California Family Code of Civil Procedure Section 2030 provides that the court may order one spouse to contribute to the attorney's fees and costs incurred by the other spouse during a marital dissolution proceeding based on each spouse's ability to pay, economic needs, and ability to secure competent representation. Such an order for contribution does not purport to determine the propriety of the fee charged a spouse by his or her own counsel. Such questions remain within the elective purview of the fee arbitration process. In addition, sometimes a client, pursuant to a contract, has the right to request that a court order the opposing party in a civil action to pay all or a portion of the client's costs, including attorney's fees incurred in the lawsuit.

Under these scenarios, clients and their counsel are working toward the same goal of recovering fees and costs from an opponent. And the court, by necessity, is not compelled to adjudicate the reasonableness of the fees charged the prevailing party by his or her own counsel. In these circumstances, recovery of attorney's fees and costs from an opponent in litigation doesn't deny a client the right to arbitrate a fee dispute with his or her attorney—because such fees are not set by "court order."

This discussion is adapted from State Bar of California Arbitration Advisory 94-2.

Section 10:

Practical Billing Considerations

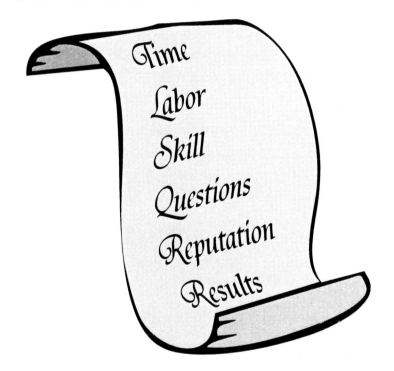

Time

Labor

Skill

Questions

Reputation

Results

All pricing is arbitrary. Whether a pharmaceutical company decides to sell a drug for hundreds of times its production cost or an automotive company decides to sell a car for below its production cost (and make it up in volume, as the ads used to say), it is the seller's decision. The seller needs to understand costs, set profit targets, and gauge market demand. This decision ultimately is simply an informed choice.

Similarly, a lawyer in any given area of practice, at any given firm, can submit a bill for services using an hourly rate, a flat fee, a contingency fee, or a mixture of these and other billing methods. Moreover, the amount and presentation of these charges can vary widely.

Defining Reasonableness

The only ethical requirement for billing, according to ABA Model Rule of Professional Conduct 1.5, is that "a lawyer shall not make an agreement for, charge, or collect an unreasonable fee." The rule defines "reasonableness" by such factors as:

- ► The time and labor required

- ► The novelty and difficulty of the questions involved

- ► The skill requisite to perform the legal service properly

- ► The customary local fee for similar services

- ► The amount involved and the results obtained

- ► The time limitations imposed by the matter

- ► The experience, reputation, and ability of the lawyer

Some of these criteria are relatively objective, particularly the time required and the customary local fees. But to a much greater extent, the rule's guidelines of how to define a reasonable fee are directly related to the value that the client receives in terms of a lawyer's skill, timeliness, experience, reputation, and results. Of course, the main purpose of billing is to make sure you get paid. But there is a secondary purpose that lawyers often miss: to leave the client with a favorable impression of the services you provided. In other words, your bill is another tool for client communication. The perfect bill is one that speaks clearly and directly to clients about how you as a lawyer have improved their lives.

Conveying Value through Detailed Billings

Lawyers should use their bills to educate clients about value. Otherwise, lawyers will have trouble using the value or alternative billing approach with clients who are not sophisticated in business matters or may not appreciate how value is measured in a transactional matter or in litigation—and who thus may not understand that the fee for value provided is reasonable. This, of course, reinforces the need for communication, trust, and rapport between client and lawyer, so you can more effectively express value in terms of units (money) or some other format or means that will be clear to the client.

Once you establish your benchmarks, you can bill in a regular and timely way, using statements that contain a full narrative of the work done and the results that

> "There are few ways a man can be more innocently employed than in getting money."
>
> – *Samuel Johnson*

work accomplished. This also allows you to provide status updates easily and to reinforce that every action you took on behalf of the client had a purpose.

Such information will help generate comprehensible billing statements that clearly list actions you have taken on the client's behalf while relating them to the time it took to realize value—simultaneously showing how hard you worked *and* what your work accomplished. This type of billing statement will go beyond a mere laundry list of tasks performed. Some items on your list may even involve actions and items noted on the bill as time increments with "no charge." This is a vivid way to let your clients know that, though your time is valuable, you value your working relationship together more.

Of course, you want to be just as detailed when setting forth what you do charge for. Too many lawyers make the mistake of brevity when billing–merely stating, for example, "worked on motion for summary judgment, 20 hours." The far better method is to break any such task and charge into its basic elements, specifying the

Sample Status Update Form

EDWARD POLL, J.D., M.B.A. Attorney at Law Suite 1200 421 Howland Canal Venice, CA 90291 Telephone: (800) 837-5880	☐ SPECIAL ☐ MONTHLY ☐ QUARTERLY ☐ SEMI-ANNUAL ☐ ANNUAL	**STATUS REPORT**	CLIENT: MATTER: FILE NO.:

We are pleased to provide you with this Report on the status of your matter. The following entries, as checked, are applicable:

TYPE OF CASE AND GENERAL PROGRESS OF MATTER:

☐ OFFICE	☐ GENERAL LITIGATION	☐ ESTATE
☐ Case Evaluation ☐ Research and Investigation ☐ Negotiation ☐ Document Drafting ☐ Closing	☐ Case Evaluation ☐ Research and Investigation ☐ Pleading ☐ Discovery ☐ Motions and Pre-Trial ☐ Final Trial Preparation ☐ Trial ☐ Post-Trial (Or Appeal)	☐ Filing Petition ☐ Assembling Assets ☐ Preparing Inventory ☐ Dealing With Claims ☐ Filing and Paying Taxes ☐ Preparing Final Account ☐ Distribution and Closing

CURRENT MATTER STATUS:

We are currently waiting for the following items: To be provided by:	Our next efforts on your behalf will be:
1. _____ ☐ You ☐ 2. _____ ☐ You ☐ 3. _____ ☐ You ☐ 4. _____ ☐ You ☐	

ACCOUNT STATUS:

The status of your account with us is presently:

☐ Current. THANK YOU.

☐ In arrears _____ months in the amount of $_____. Please remit or make arrangements to settle this account.

☐ We need a further deposit of $_____ into our Trust Account.

OTHER NOTES:

Thank you,

Dated: _____, _____   Edward Poll

Form generously contributed by Wesley P. Hackett, Jr. All Rights Reserved.

amount of time each element required–for example: "reviewed key documents and deposition testimony, 6 hours"; "drafted a statement of uncontested facts as required by court procedure, 3 hours"; "researched precedents in four similar cases, 2 hours"; and so on.

Detailed itemization doesn't try clients' patience—it helps them understand just how much you did for them. Be sure to use action verbs to describe your services. And clearly indicate the specifics of what you accomplished. This gives clients an appreciation of the effort required for success.

Increasing Convenience

You should also make bills easy to receive and pay by taking advantage of all that technology affords. One simple way to do this is to e-mail bills as PDF files, rather than sending bills through the postal mail. The increased speed and convenience of delivering bills via e-mail often results in quicker payment. (Note though, that you need to ensure PDFs are not modified with the latest software after they leave your office).

For corporate clients, consider using an electronic invoicing service. A billing service requires substantial initial setup and coordination and is mainly justified for larger clients. But once it has been set up, an electronic billing service can perform much of the routine work of certifying compliance with the client's billing rules and assigning fees and costs by matter handled and by lawyer. Finally, you should afford clients of any size the ultimate convenience of paying the bill by credit card.

Value versus Time

Regardless of the billing methodology that is chosen, any lawyer is safer by keeping track of time expended. In case your billings are ever questioned, either by a judge needing to approve the fee or by an arbitration panel in a fee dispute, the clearest tried-and-true way to demonstrate what you've done usually comes back to hourly metrics.

If a client agrees to value billing, why should it matter whether a lawyer keeps track of time? The answer comes back to defining a fee as "reasonable." If a client wants to dispute whether a value charge for a service was reasonable, a time record can provide useful backup documentation. However, no lawyer should ever let it come to that.

If the client pays each bill every month like clockwork, your relationship is working. But if the client owes money and shows little inclination to pay it, the lawyer-client relationship is clearly on the rocks and the client likely thinks your fee is unreasonable. You truly have a good relationship with your client only when the client's account receivable is up to date. Delinquent accounts indicate that the client doesn't respect you, is attempting to hoodwink or undercut you, or is dissatisfied and considering disciplinary action against you.

Section 11:

The Collections Process

Several years ago, when the 300-lawyer global law firm Altheimer & Gray was forced to file for bankruptcy, a very important fact got little attention: The firm had accumulated $30 million in outstanding accounts receivable. Had the firm been more diligent and aggressive about collecting the money it was owed, it might

---

have remained alive. Other law firms have had similar experiences. Steve Finley, founder of Finley Kumble (generally credited with being the first megafirm before it disintegrated in the late 1980s), contended that firm's demise began with a new managing partner who was not so aggressive as Finley had been about collecting receivables.

The importance of collecting the money you are owed could not be more obvious for large law firms and sole practitioners alike. And yet this lesson remains hard for lawyers to grasp. The truth is that a lawyer's inventory is not billable hours—instead, it is the *cash* those hours represent. Although most lawyers understand the need to win client work and to perform it effectively, they are uncomfortable with pursuing client payment. The result can be bounced checks, missed payrolls, and—ultimately—insolvency.

Measuring Collections Performance

There are two fundamental measurements of law firm financial performance that relate to the important issue of getting paid:

- ► Realization—being the amount of a lawyer's time actually billed and collected

- ► Collection rate—being the speed at which billable work is turned into cash receipts

Realization is sometimes discussed in two levels:

1. The percent of billable or booked hours billed (billed-to-billable ratio)

2. The percent of billed work collected (collected-to-billed ratio)

The goal is to bill all the work you do and get paid for all the work you bill. An overall ratio of less than 90 percent is a recipe for trouble. An overall ratio of greater than 95 percent, which indicates your clients are paying promptly, may be the result of you clearly communicating your value—*or* it may mean that your rates are too low.

Assessing Client Responses

If you defined your payment terms up front in the engagement letter and the client has not lived up to those terms, it's symptomatic of a deeper communications problem—and you, the lawyer, must work with the client to resolve the problem. Typically there are five reasons clients fail to pay their bills:

- ▸ They didn't receive a bill or statement.

- ▸ They didn't understand your bill, what you did for them, or the value of what you did for them.

- ▸ They didn't ask you to do what you billed them for.

- ▸ Their cash flow is temporarily interrupted, despite their best intentions to pay quickly.

- ▸ Their business has "gone south" and they can't afford to pay you.

Better communication can prevent or manage each of these problems. The first three problems require the lawyer to focus more on each client's awareness of and response to the billing and collection process. The last two require the lawyer to learn about and be more sensitive to the client's needs and conditions. None of this requires constant calls or elaborate questionnaires. You should simply meet informally with the client (perhaps over coffee) and ask, "How are you doing? Did you understand my bill? Is there an issue that concerns you? Is there something I can help you with?" Given this opportunity, the client will usually provide you with honest answers—and if there's a problem, it's better to learn now than to keep haggling over an unpaid bill.

Setting the Terms

The "Terms of Engagement" subsection of Section 2, "The Engagement Letter," sets out at length the importance of defining collection terms. The lesson bears repeating here. Lawyers can control fees collection to a greater degree than they usually believe is possible. When an attorney agrees to perform services for a client, the lawyer *and* the client are entering into a two-way bargain: The lawyer agrees to perform to the best of his or her ability in accordance with professional standards, and the client agrees to communicate and cooperate fully—which includes paying the bill.

At a minimum, both lawyer and client should agree to the following points regarding payment and collection in the engagement letter:

- The scope of the representation—i.e., what the lawyer will and will not do

- The fee to be charged

- How the fee will be calculated

- When the fee is to be paid

- The consequences of nonpayment, including the lawyer's right to withdraw

- Budgeting and staffing

- Frequency and method of communications from lawyer to client

- The client's responsibilities, including payment in accordance with the agreement

- Dispute resolution procedures if either party has a disagreement about the fee

Stipulating payment rates and terms up front is the best way to get paid. This is particularly true if you prepare a budget that addresses events, time, and anticipated fees and you get your client to accept it. That increases the chances of collecting your fee significantly because the client understands what to expect. The engagement letter should state explicitly that you will stay in continual touch with the client about expenses versus budget.

Maintaining the Relationship

If the client pays each bill every month like clockwork, the relationship is working. If, however, the client owes a great deal of money and shows little inclination to pay it, the relationship is clearly on the rocks. Shared expectations, effective communication, and dependable follow-through by lawyer and client all define the kind of good relationship that results in collecting a higher percentage of your billings. These issues are inextricably tied together, despite what some lawyers think.

If clients have the ability to pay but are not paying, it is likely that they're unhappy with some aspect of the representation and are choosing to express it by slowing down or stopping the payment schedule. To avoid such a situation, regularly communicate with the client about progress according to the budget. Make note of any additional time and expenses that may be incurred. If a payment slowdown does take place and you suspect it is due to client dissatisfaction, again, talk with the client about what the issue is.

Knowing When to Walk Away

In large firms, when such a troubled client relationship develops, the overall cost of an individual bad debt to each partner is minimal. Lawyers in small firms or sole practices, on the other hand, see an immediate reduction in take-home pay. But regardless of firm size, lawyers of all stripes too often continue working for nonpaying clients in a misguided hope that continuing the relationship means ultimately

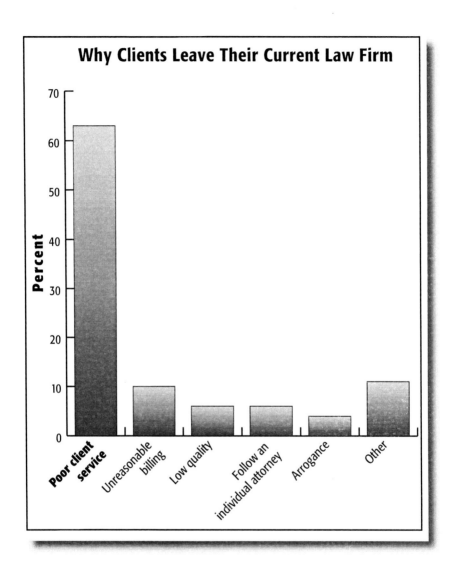

Why Clients Leave Their Current Law Firm

getting paid and receiving referrals in the future. The truth, however, is that clients respect firmness and a businesslike approach and generally won't go out of their way for lawyers they disrespect.

So what is your recourse when a fee payment impasse develops? A lawyer cannot ethically cease representation when the client will be prejudiced—for example, by withdrawing within 60 days of a court date. However, ABA Model Rule 1.16 ("Declining or Terminating Representation") allows lawyers to withdraw if "the client fails substantially to fulfill an obligation to the lawyer regarding the lawyer's services and has been given reasonable warning that the lawyer will withdraw unless the obligation is fulfilled." So take note: If you try to withdraw without adequate communication on and careful records of the client's billing and payment performance, the result may be a state bar disciplinary action requiring future "involuntary servitude" (or *pro bono* work) to fulfill your ethical obligations toward the client.

Keeping Track

You must have a policy that details how to keep track of clients' payments and how to contact clients when they are late with payments. You want to review your accounts receivable weekly and determine which clients are behind on their payments. Forgetting or ignoring "old" clients results in forgetting or ignoring the accounts receivable as well. This results in a failure to collect your money, so remembering to track old open accounts is vital. On the one hand, you will be able to pursue collection with the regular, weekly reminders that money is owed to you. (The "you" in this context is the firm). On the other hand, you will be able to thank a client who has paid, the kind of courtesy that pays off in increased goodwill.

Someone on your staff who's good with people and sensitive to their needs should make the reminder call. That way, clients won't be confused about whether the call is to request information needed for their matter or to seek payment. The lawyer should make this call only when he or she is prepared to "fire" the client if the client fails to bring the account current.[*]

If necessary, use a collection service. There are certainly ethical snares involved, but you can avoid them by disclosing to a collection service only those details that are absolutely necessary for them to do their job *without* jeopardizing client confidentiality. Moreover, it is a given that a collection effort should not be made unless you have reviewed the client file and ensured that there is no negligence on your part. Peer review of your file may be appropriate here.

One study shows that a bill that is over 60 days past due can still be collected about 89 percent of the time. However, that drops to a 67 percent likelihood of collection after six months, and to a 45 percent likelihood after one year. Thus, promptly identifying who is not paying their bills lets you take immediate and appropriate action. Unlike good wine, an account receivable does not get better with age.

---

[*] For more on this topic, see Ed Poll's book *Collecting Your Fee: Getting Paid from Intake to Invoice*, published by the American Bar Association (2003).

Detailing Your Collections Policy

Your collections policy should cover in usable electronic form everything from the beginning of the client relationship to the payment of the final bill. Hire a collections manager or designate a staff person to handle all details of the collections policy, including these:

- ► Credit terms, including when to inquire about unpaid balances and when to cease work if payment stops

- ► A sample fee agreement, to be modified as necessary

- ► Collection terms, including guidelines on when and how to engage a collection agency

- ► Incentives for lawyers to have a high collection percentage on the fees they bill (the realization rate) and enforcement actions against those partners who lag on collections (such as withholding compensation or deducting collection expenses from it)

Resolving Disputes

Consistent with the Rules of Professional Conduct, you should stop work for clients who do not pay. That step will focus the client's attention on the problem. Ask the client what he or she would like you to do to resolve the billing dispute, and listen carefully to what the client suggests in response. Generally, price is not the issue with most clients. Therefore, lawyers should

Ask the client what he or she would like you to do to resolve the billing dispute, and listen carefully to what the client suggests in response. Generally, price is not the issue with most clients.

resist discounting their fees. However, in a collection situation, it is important to do whatever is necessary to resolve the conflict. Clients who argue about overbilling are often just angling for a discounted bill. If, after all other efforts to collect have been exhausted, the client is merely interested in a fee discount, give it. Do it to get rid of the matter—and the client. That way you are not paying collections staff to keep flogging the matter, and you are much less likely to be sued for malpractice.

However, if the client earlier agreed to pay the full amount, do not cut the fee later. This sort of price shenanigan is quite popular during the month of December with clients of large law firms. Such clients agree to pay their large bills in order to wangle huge discounts because the remuneration system for partners is based on how much has been collected by the year's end. Any bills collected in January do not count for another 11 months. Some of these clients, unfortunately, have gotten into the habit of attempting to obtain discounts on their lawyers' fees for every matter.

Ending Discounts

If a firm is truly determined to get away from offering some type of discount, clients may well resist—especially if the firm's past practice leads them to believe, "I'll just wait until the end of the year and I know I'll receive a discount at that time." There are a number of ways to stop this practice—some are better than others, but all certainly practical. Alternatives include doing any of the following:

- ► Offer the discount immediately to get outstanding bills paid, emphasizing that subsequently there will be no more discounting in December or any other month—and mean it.

- ► Refuse to offer the discount in December, telling clients that there is a fee agreement in place and it will be enforced, irrespective of the firm's failure to enforce it in the past.

- ► Tell clients that unless they honor the agreement that they accepted and signed, the firm will not continue to work for them—which Model Rule 1.16 permits. Advise them that they should obtain other counsel and that the firm will seek to enforce collection of all billed fees outstanding.

- ► Offer a discount for everything to date and make it interesting for the client with the proviso that all work *hereafter* will be billed at full rate and collected in accordance with the fee agreement. Get the client's full acknowledgement of both the discount acceptance and the future adherence to the fee agreement.

- ▶ Accept the discount process and admit to yourself that instead of getting 100 percent, you're receiving only 75 percent (or whatever figure)—*and* then compensate by raising the fee or rate either higher or sooner than otherwise would have been the case.

Each of these options for breaking the discounting cycle says that the firm is a business with certain policies in place—*and* that you are willing to treat clients fairly when they treat you well.

Getting Paid Faster

In addition to all the strategic collection ideas discussed up to this point, there are additional tactics that any firm can take to get fees paid and into the bank quickly. Here are just three examples of innovative tactical tools that any firm can use.

Firms are taking advantage of the new check scanners offered by banks to more quickly and securely deposit client checks. Scanners treat a check virtually as a debit card, making deposit instantaneous. A related but more comprehensive strategy is to negotiate for a lockbox with the bank. Many banks advertise this as one of their premier business services. In this arrangement, the bank picks up remittances several times a day, records them, and sends details of the transaction to you, as the bank's customer. Modern technology allows the bank to communicate this information on the same day as the deposit, or on the day following the deposit. This saves time otherwise needed to open the mail and process the deposit.

More firms are closing their billing on the 25th day of each month to get their bills into the "first of the month" billing cycle of clients—both businesses and individuals. I've long advocated that law firms develop alternatives to diversify their receivables stream. Sending out invoices on or about the 25th of the month is a good example. This strategy shortens the receivables stream because clients receive statements on or before the first day of the following month. Because most people pay their bills on or about the first of the month, a bill that comes after that date is frequently kept for payment until the following month. Another idea is to stagger client billings by billing one-fourth of the alphabet each week. In this way, the firm receives money from one-fourth of its clients weekly, rather than all once per month, which evens out cash flow over the month.

To pressure partners to collect bills sooner, firms are using automated e-mail reminders and other added features in their time-and-billing programs to keep the pressure on automatically. This is certainly good internal policy. But, as noted earlier, firms can take it further by applying technology to external client billings by e-mailing bills as PDF files, or using an electronic invoicing service, and also by accepting credit card payments. However note that the latest technology does allow for recipient modification of PDF files, so you must take care to ensure the conformity of the original bill to the PDF version sent.

The bottom line is that it should now be apparent that collecting your fees is an active process—and a vital one. It is the last step that closes the circle in any engagement and results in the "balance" of The 3-Dimensional Lawyer™ approach. The agreement between client and lawyer simply isn't complete until you get paid. The process only works when you take charge and make it work.

Section 12:

The Role of Compensation Systems

There is little doubt that compensation at the nation's largest law firms is on an unbroken upward trend. Recent numbers for the 100 largest American law firms show that average profits per partner topped $1 million in 2005 for the first time. Per-partner compensation rates reflect these firms' high profitability levels.

The contrast to the typical lawyer's experience is dramatic. In reporting on the megafirm profit numbers, *USA Today* quoted a professor at Loyola University Law School as saying, "The average [American] lawyer is working at a small firm making $60,000 to $100,000 a year. Even at large firms in [many] big cities, it's $100,000 to $160,000 on average." In California, the largest state, data indicate that one-quarter of all lawyers—who are typically in small and solo practices—earn $50,000 or less per year, and a total of 50 percent earn only $100,000 per year or less.

Of course, per-partner profits are in no small way tied to the fees the lawyers charge—and whether clients will pay that fee because they feel the service they receive is worth it.

Profits and Rates

Whether it's $1,000 or $100 an hour, the rates that lawyers set depend on a number of factors, including the following:

- Years of experience (i.e., more years out of law school generally means a higher billing rate)

- Practice area (e.g., mergers and acquisitions work is valued higher than family law)

- Geographic locale (e.g., lawyers in Manhattan charge more than those in Des Moines)

- Number of lawyers competing in the same geographic and practice areas (i.e., the more lawyers, the higher the competitive pressure on pricing)

- Type of billing method (be it hourly rate, flat fee, contingency fee, and so on)

Ultimately, though, the rate that most lawyers charge is based on their "gut feel" after evaluating these and other factors. Rate setting is definitely an art, not a science.

Implicit in all of this is the presumed law firm interrelationship between billings, profits and compensation. But is this really the standard model? Should it be?

Consider a firm in which one of the highest paid · partners did very little billing. The reason was she served as an office managing partner and was compensated on the basis of the office's *overall* performance—which, among other things, reflected the fact that she leveraged associates to do more billing on higher value work. Everyone in the firm benefited. This is just one anecdote that brings into question some of the conventional wisdom about law firm compensation systems.

Fair Compensation and Firm Culture

There are, of course, various formulae for determining compensation among partners. One might suggest, however, that it's not important *what* formula is used as long as all involved perceive that the process of determining the numbers is fair. Or put differently, the system needs to recognize that people respond to what they're rewarded for.

It's also worth suggesting that people will accept a great deal less than the top compensation as long as they genuinely like the environment in which they work. While compensation needs to be competitive (it need not be on the high end), firm culture has a far greater impact than money for a great many professionals today. People deeply want to like the work they do and those with whom they do it. Moreover, lawyers who are together in an office

> **People deeply want to like the work they do and those with whom they do it.**

environment should share a camaraderie that shapes the development of the firm culture. Many factors come into play, including the exchange of ideas and collegial education of one lawyer by another. These are vital to the success of the firm and its individual members, too.

Now, let's apply this concept to law firm compensation by considering two typical compensation models: (1) lockstep, in which the firm's overall success each year is averaged out to determine a standard rate of compensation increase for most lawyers; and (2) "eat what you kill (EWYK)," in which all lawyers are rewarded based on how much business they personally bring in. Each of these models has advantages and disadvantages, which are admirably summed up by consultant Bruce MacEwen in his online publication on law firm economics, "Adam Smith, Esq.":

- ► Lockstep is good at building collaboration, client service teams, and institutionalizing clients

- ► Lockstep is bad at rewarding exceptional performers and penalizing subpar performers

- ► EWYK is good at developing new business and new markets, and spurring entrepreneurship

- ► EWYK is bad at cross-selling services and promoting firm harmony

Obviously there are positives in each approach, but MacEwen pinpoints perhaps the important distinction between the two:

> *There is a genuine intangible value in a sense of collegiality in the workplace, in team-building, in delivering top-notch service untainted by self interest, in contributing to an institution—"The Firm" —over an extended period of one's career, and not least in avoiding the infighting, neck-biting, and generally deplorable "Lord of the Flies" behavior associated with arguing over such nasty details as origination credits.*

So, any firm that encourages lawyers to maximize their individual compensation may have fast near-term growth. At the same time, approaching compensation as an institution makes for greater firm harmony and longevity. But the problem is that both lockstep and EWYK systems generally depend on the same metrics: hours worked per year, origination credit, supervision credit, and other formulaic measures based on the billable hour. And that is not where the money is.

The Corporate Model: Value-Driven Work and Compensation

Traditional law firm compensation models overemphasize billable hours. For the largest law firms and solo practices alike, collecting the money you are owed—meaning your realization rate—is far more important than the number of hours you bill. Remember, your real inventory is not billed hours—it's the collected cash those hours represent. And ultimately, promoting teamwork and cooperation between its lawyers can help any firm increase collections.

However, promoting the kind of team effort that increases collections requires changing to a more cooperative corporate compensation model that depends on the *entire* organization's success. It means tying base compensation to the effectiveness of involving other firm lawyers as part of the team delivering legal services to clients. To illustrate, in the firm mentioned earlier, where the highly paid managing partner did little direct billing, the compensation formula is based on an office/practice group profit center model. Each profit center is headed by a managing partner, who receives the percentage of the firm's overall profits that the profit center generates and divides it among profit center members according to certain flexible parameters. This is the corporate model, which says that compensation is paid based on what is generated for *the organization*—not for any one individual.

To be clear, a firm's size doesn't necessarily reflect on either revenue per partner or profit per partner. As an example, the Los Angeles firm Irell & Manella has total revenue one-tenth that of the largest firms (so it doesn't qualify for inclusion in the AmLaw 100), yet it has controlled its leverage such that its revenue per lawyer and profit per partner would rank near the top of AmLaw 100 firms.

Another aspect of the corporate model relates to how firms grow in tandem with their clients and their marketplace. To succeed long term, firms need

Promoting the kind of team effort that increases collections requires changing to a more cooperative corporate compensation model that depends on the *entire* organization's success. It means tying base compensation to the effectiveness of involving other firm lawyers as part of the team delivering legal services to clients.

to look for clients who have good growth potential. Compared to routine commodity-type legal work, more highly focused and "high-end" work will result in greater revenue and more profitable growth. And when clients perceive the work of the firm as having high value, then the firm can charge more, even a percentage of the value of the work. This shifts the billing perspective from one of time (the hourly rate) to one of value, where the profits are significantly higher. It's simple Business 101, although a lesson too many firms ignore.

Importantly, the corporate compensation model supports this kind of work because it reflects the approach of corporate clients themselves. Corporate clients live in a world that favors and rewards continuous improvement and they are quite willing to pay for quality work—but they will *not* pay for the inefficiency, duplicated efforts, and waste of time that occurs when lawyers in the same firm compete against each other. Thus, while the "star system" that rewards the individuals who stand out from the crowd results in a few highly compensated individuals, it also inhibits the institutionalization of the firm and its long-term success.

Bottom line: If a law firm wants to promote teamwork and "partnering" among its members, the firm culture and compensation system must change to a more cooperative corporate model. The compensation committee or the managing partner must affirmatively state that a requirement of being a member of the firm is that other members of the firm be involved in all matters involving x dollars' exposure, minimum expected attorney's fees, or certain types of cases, and the like. Base compensation must then, in some fashion, be tied to lawyers' effectiveness in delivering client services as an organizational team. As this approach expands, the firm can also shift the emphasis of its recognition programs from individual to team rewards. Even individual rewards should acknowledge people who are effective team players, freely sharing their expertise. The fairest compensation approach gets away from a star system that rewards only the individuals who stand out from the crowd by also rewarding those individuals who help the crowd perform better.

Pro Bono Issues

In addition, to be truly effective, any type of compensation system should track and give compensation recognition for nonbillable services provided by the lawyers—whether this means pro bono representation, involvement in professional associations, community service activities, or some other use of lawyer time that is not directly billable client work.

Pro bono is probably easiest to define: the delivery of legal services to persons of limited means and to charitable, religious, civic, community, governmental, and educational organizations that serve those people. Although lawyers regularly engage in many civic and charitable activities, by volunteering, serving on bar association committees and boards of nonprofit organizations, and otherwise contributing to their communities, many firms do not track and give credit for such activity.

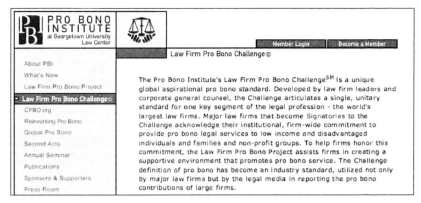

The Pro Bono Institute, at www.probonoinst.org, is a nonprofit organization that provides research, consultative services, analysis and assessment, publications, and training to a broad range of legal audiences.

Nearly 15 years ago the American Bar Association and the Pro Bono Institute, housed at the Georgetown University Law Center, launched the "Law Firm Pro Bono Challenge." This program specifically seeks larger firms (those with more than 50 lawyers) to become signators and make an institutional commitment to pro bono service. It offers a progressive and ambitious performance standard: a target of either 3 or 5 percent of each firm's total billable hours, in addition to the hours-per-attorney standard commonly used in articulating pro bono goals. (While firms have the option to select an alternative goal of 60 or 100 hours per attorney, virtually all signatory firms have elected to use the preferred percentage goals.) By promoting a percentage goal, the Pro Bono Challenge program ties pro bono activity to firm productivity and profitability.

Of course, organizational profitability is ultimately the key to successful pro bono performance in any firm. If the client billings are not sufficient to support pro bono work, the commitment to serving the public will be tenuous at best. This makes the concept of firmwide team building an even larger issue. Certainly an institutional pro bono target can best be met under a corporate compensation model, where all share in the firm's performance. But for a solo practice or a megafirm, strong financial performance is the foundation that supports making a meaningful pro bono effort.

Section 13:

Associate Compensation Issues

Partner compensation is central to most considerations about billing in law firms. However, what about associates, who contribute both billable time and leverage for their firms, but in many cases do not have direct client relationships? They, too, are an important part of a firm's value and profitablity equation.

Associate P&L Calculation

A personal note illustrates the basic compensation conundrum of associates. When I was a law firm associate, I had a conversation with the managing partner. I showed him what my percentage of the firm's billings was, what my expense to the firm was, and what my "profit" to the firm was (though I had no clue about my realization rate). After getting over the shock that I would attempt to have that information, he asked me why I kept it. I told him that I enjoyed my job and wanted to retain it, and I knew the firm's partners wouldn't keep me if I weren't profitable for them. I didn't need to be profitable every month, but I needed to be profitable for the year. Shortly after that discussion, I was invited to become a partner.

Ideally, associates should have available the information to determine their own profit and loss (P&L) in order to enhance their worth to the firm. The information would include:

- ▸ Their billable hours, for the latest month and year to date

- ▸ How many hours the firm billed out for them, compared to markdowns or write-offs for some of the work (individually or as an average percentage applied to all associates)

- ▸ Direct expenses for compensation (including bonus and benefits), clerical help, technology, office space, and the like

- ▸ Indirect expenses, or overhead (percentage of rent, insurance, utilities, entertainment, and education that each associate accounts for)

Sample P&L Worksheet for Associates

Billings	
Number of hours recorded	
or Number of hours submitted for billing	
x Hourly billing rate	
Total:	
Direct Expenses	
Associate's compensation, including: • Salary • Employer taxes (@ 30% cost to the firm) • Profit-sharing and pension plan contributions • Health insurance • Travel allowance • Miscellaneous	
Secretary's salary and employment taxes (@ pro rata based on number of lawyers sharing the secretary's services)	
Rent (@ pro rata based on price per square foot)	
Other direct expenses	
Total:	
Indirect Expenses	
Office overhead (common area rent, insurance, utilities, entertainment, education, etc., @ firm's lawyer overhead percentage)	
Total:	

The result should determine an individual net profit value to the firm:

Billings – [Associate's Total Compensation + Direct and Indirect Expenses] = Net Profit for the Firm

Few associates at larger firms have access to all the numbers for this calculation, but the accounting department may provide many of the numbers and educated guesses can be made for the rest.

Profitability versus Pay

Associate profitability has come particularly to the fore, as average first-year associate salaries at some New York megafirms have exploded to $160,000 and beyond. Some commentators say this opens up tremendous opportunity for smaller firms with a more rational pay structure. General counsel at company after company declare that they will not pay for such outrageous salaries when it comes to *their* legal work.

However, with the competition for top law school talent so fierce, and with profits per partner at the 100 largest firms averaging more than $1 million annually, it's a given that the cost of legal talent is bound to rise yet more. What starts in New York will move to Chicago and San Francisco and elsewhere. And while associate salaries may be high, if compared to equity partners' revenue, the percentage is actually lower today than it was only a few years ago. If associates are making so much money, partners are, too.

So what about the corporate clients' insistence that they won't pay such high rates for beginners? The simple fact is that, if they stay with their megafirms, their option is to pay for senior associates making $500,000 a year and partners making $1 million or more. What I think these clients are really saying is they don't want to pay for the on-the-job education of beginning associates—but the truth is there is no such thing as apprenticeship training for U.S. law school graduates. They obtain their J.D. degrees and move right into practice. Both law firms and clients have the economic incentive to use these lawyers right away, and from the law firm's perspective, it is imperative to do so. If these young lawyers have no practical experience and aren't trained on the job, where will future senior associates and partners come from?

The Role of Leverage

High associate compensation is made possible by the magic of leverage. Consider a recent NALP study of law firm leverage nationwide from 1995 to 2006, which showed that leverage has returned to levels of the mid-1990s. After reaching a high of 1.16 associates to partners in 2002, the figure was down to 0.99 in 2006. Thus, on a national average, law firms paid more for the work being done per hour. Failure to use leverage invariably increases costs of operation.

Such a failure is untenable in today's megafirms when the average profit per partner at the 100 largest firms has passed the $1 million mark and the top 10 firms book a profit per partner of $2 million or more. To sustain and expand such financial performance, these firms must leverage lower paid associates and cut ties to higher paid but underperforming partners, as several firms have recently done under highly publicized circumstances. Such partners were "retired" or otherwise laid off when their firm's *overall* strategic goal for profitability was not being met. Despite the furor, this is a legitimate rearrangement of organizational structures to impact accounting metrics. Why should law firms, now playing in the big leagues with revenues approaching $1 billion, be exempt from the same decisions that face their large corporate clients?

Recruiting Costs and Compensation

Recruiting new lawyers is a special cost situation because the firm's current lawyers often are directly involved in the process. Consider this hypothetical example. New lawyer "A" is earning $160,000; he was hired through a search firm whose fee is 25 percent of the first year's compensation package, or in this case $40,000. (If you're in a large firm, you may not use a search firm but will, instead, have higher lawyer involvement and thus higher recruiting costs anyway.)

Assume further that the firm is somewhat progressive and has an education program that helps the new lawyer assimilate into the firm culture—in this case, the training time is 100 hours for the associate at a billable rate of $200 per hour, or $20,000. And don't forget the cost of the partners doing the training, which let's say is 100 hours at the partner's rate of $500 per hour, or $50,000. Assume still further that partners spend time in recruiting and interviewing

Why should law firms, now playing in the big leagues with revenues approaching $1 billion, be exempt from the same decisions that face their large corporate clients?

the new lawyer to the tune of 50 hours at their billable rate of $500 per hour, for an additional $25,000 in costs.

Without considering reduced productivity in the beginning when the lawyer new to the firm first gets started, or the cost to the firm of disruption, retraining, and client concern when another lawyer is assigned to his or her matter in "midstream," the cost to the firm during the first year of employment is already $295,000. This is hugely expensive—and becomes more so if the lawyer leaves.

I have always had difficulty understanding the large firm managing partner who once said that the "culling process" and resulting revolving door of young associates was "normal and acceptable." Experience, on the contrary, shows that more care in the initial phases of recruiting and training will lower the high cost of this "turnstile" and increase overall profits, not to mention the increase in lawyer satisfaction.

For all these reasons, it only makes practical business sense for firms to treat associates with the same care that they use in hiring them. If firms want to strengthen their performance and value to clients, hiring the right person for the right job the first time will create more profits. The most effective way to do that is to provide extensive education for new lawyers to improve their skills and then involve them in the firm's financial and organizational life so they understand and appreciate their role and look forward to their future with the firm. That is the path to career satisfaction—and to firm profitability. It is also the path to increasing client satisfaction and lowering overall legal costs.

Admittedly, this discussion has focused mainly on large law firms. There is, of course, another segment of the profession, the vast majority who make up more than 70 percent of the private practitioners in this country. For this group, compensation is significantly lower. In fact, some surveys in California, New York, and elsewhere indicate that many private practitioners earn less than $100,000. Obviously, these lawyers face significant price/revenue pressures from their clients. In these firms, too, both partners and associates should analyze their practices from the perspective of The Business of Law® and seek continuous improvement, just like successful corporate clients do.

Section 14:

The Dynamics in Action

Years ago I registered the phrase "The Business of Law®" because it summarized the basics of my law firm consultancy and because it also summarized such an important truth—one that many lawyers seemingly still fail to understand. Yet nothing is more important to the future of law firms than conducting themselves like businesses and seeing the implications of how fees, collections, and compensation interact—implications we have analyzed in this report. This concept is at the heart of a firm's financial life and dramatically affects the firm's relationships with its clients.

Commoditization

In recent years convergence and commoditization—the "Two Cs"—have become major issues for large regional and national law firms. Convergence is the trend among large corporate clients to reduce their legal expenses by paring down to a few dozen or less the hundreds of outside law firms that they previously used. The survivors of these parings are frequently expected to provide certain kinds of work with relatively steady volume (such as patent filings or employment litigation) at fixed rates over a certain period of time, turning these matters into the legal equivalent of a commodity. With commoditized services, lawyers focus on specific targets, such as settling cases for the lowest legal cost and settlement amount where warranted.

The hard truth is that commoditization is also increasingly an issue for small firm and sole practitioners, too, particularly in areas such as wills, bankruptcy filings, and divorces. Spend some time on the Internet and you'll see a whole host of services in such areas that are targeted at individual consumers and being offered by lawyers at low fixed prices. There are even software packages claiming to make the purchasers their own lawyer in these practice areas. I'm reminded of the H&R Block television commercial showing a husband preparing the family tax return. He is stuck. His wife approaches him and suggests that he ask "the box" for help. You know, of course, the answer from the box: Silence. Then a voiceover says that help from H&R Block is only a phone call away.

Essentially, low-price pitches meet with success because too many lawyers have done a poor job of addressing the value and benefits they bring to these matters—the worth, as opposed to the cost, of the services provided.

Productization

The legal services we provide should be seen as unique because of the attorney-client relationship, or because a special skill is required to deal with the given challenge, or because the client has a particular constraint that only a few lawyers can accept. Yet when clients increasingly want to see the dynamic shift toward the commodity model, the momentum can be hard to resist, at least completely. So what type of options do lawyers have in response?

One way is to consider "productizing" your practice by providing a tangible product that opens the door to the *intangible*, value-added services you want to offer. For example, an estate planning lawyer might combat do-it-yourself Web sites and software by establishing a password-protected section on his or her firm Web site that has authoritative forms and research that the lawyer has prepared or evaluated. For a flat fee of

$100 a "client" could access this material and draw from it at will. However, if the client has a question or problem that the materials do not answer, the lawyer is available to provide personalized counsel, perhaps at a special rate that recognizes the relationship established through the Web site.

Another example might be a blog that, for a subscription fee, combines the lawyer's observations on breaking legal or regulatory issues with specialized content and research—again, with the option of asking specific questions outside of the access fee. There are numerous value-added offerings you might create based on your practice area and target market. And that's just what many creative lawyers and firms are currently considering or actually doing.

The Service-Driven Modality

The fact is, commodity work does not result in high and profitable growth unless you have a genuinely substantial volume of such work. As stated elsewhere in this report, highly focused and high-end work for clients with growth potential is what truly results in higher revenue and profits. When the client perceives the work you do as having high value, you will be able to charge more, even a percentage of the value of the work. This will get you out of the time modality of billing and into the value modality of billing where the profits are significantly higher.

The solution for the profession is to get paid for the real value and expertise that lawyers bring to clients. (See Section 5 on "Value Billing.") Clients consult a lawyer because they need help with a problem that they cannot resolve on their own. But also when it comes to a lawyer, clients value what any person values in a plumber, a doctor, or other service provider: Show up on time, do what you say you will do, finish what you start, and say please and thank you.

These traits were emphasized by the results of a Robert Half Legal Placement survey, reported in a recent issue of *The Lawyer's Competitive Edge*. The survey asked a cross-section of lawyers this question: "When clients are deciding whether or not to continue working with your firm, which one of the following attributes or considerations would you say ranks highest on their priority list?" Here is the resulting ranking:

1.	Reliability/trust	45%
2.	Relationship with client	20%
3.	Industry-specific knowledge	14%
4.	Timeliness/meeting deadlines	9%
5.	Billing rates	7%
6.	Diversity at your firm	1%
7.	Other/don't know	4%

This list is consistent with the basics of value billing. In other words, reliability and trust (expressed as "do what you say," "finish what you start," and so on) are the most important priorities. Note that billing rates are near the bottom of the list, and that cutting-edge legal advice isn't even cited.

The Functional Interaction

So what does the value concept mean for the firm's profitability? While collections are the foundation of a firm's financial performance, they are still inseparable from a number of other performance factors that determine profitability, including the following:

- Billing rates—whether hourly, blended (an average), fixed, or another measure

- Utilization—the percentage of a workweek (usually expressed as an annual average) that a lawyer actually bills

- Realization—the amount of time actually billed and collected

- Leverage—defined as the ratio of non-partners (associates, paralegals, and staff) to partners

- Expenses—related to both operations and compensation, as a percent of revenues

Of course, it's one thing to identify these financial variables and quite another for most firms to keep track of them. Today's financial information systems and software can and do produce far more information than an attorney can use or assimilate intelligently. Perhaps the only practical approach to understanding a firm's finances is to look at several broad measures.

First and foremost is the development of a cash flow statement. You need to prepare a forward-looking budget of cash receipts and payments for the next 12 months. Keep that statement on a rolling 12-month cycle, such that as you conclude the current month, you look at the 12th month and add it into your budget, adjusting all the other months as needed based on new information. As part of this process, relating back to collections, keep your accounts receivable listing always at your elbow to make sure that your clients are paying you in accordance with their agreements. If you do these two things, you will be far ahead of the financial curve compared to most firms.

Then, when you get to the point of adding up the numbers, there are two basic methods for keeping track of law firm financial performance: (1) accrual accounting and (2) cash accounting. Accrual records reflect income and expenses irrespective of whether billings have been collected or expenses paid. In other

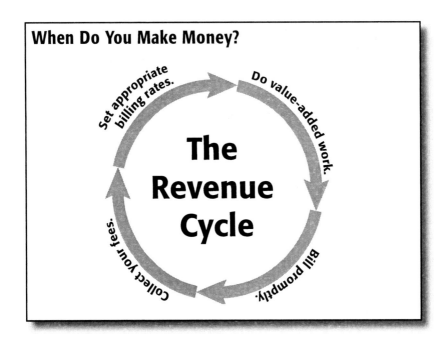

When Do You Make Money?

Set appropriate billing rates.

Do value-added work.

The Revenue Cycle

Bill promptly.

Collect your fees.

> The solution for the profession is to get paid for the real value and expertise that lawyers bring to clients.

words, accrual accounting reflects billings, work-in-progress (completed but not yet billed) and accounts receivable (work billed but not yet collected), and expenses incurred (but not yet paid).

Cash accounting, on the other hand, reflects only collections, never billings or work-in-progress and expenses actually paid. Almost all small firms operate on a cash basis, accounting for cash as it comes in and goes out. Larger firms maintain both cash and accrual records.

In addition, income statements, also called profit and loss (P&L) statements, will tell how well the firm did financially in a given period of time. Income statements often use the accrual method to tell how much revenue has been billed, how much expense has been accrued, and how much net income or profit resulted. Income or profit figures generally have little relevance to small law firms, though. Again, small firms typically operate on a cash basis, with the lawyer's salary or draw coming from positive cash flow, not from "income."

From Good Work to Cold Hard Cash

There are many more reports and metrics that firms can use to assess profitability, and this report's final section ("Getting More Information") will steer you toward resources in that regard. But no matter what yardsticks you use, financial performance for any size firm still depends on the collections function. Survey data indicate that it takes between 120 to 150 days—as much as five months—for the average law firm to turn billable hours into cash. This means that a typical small firm should have funds sufficient to operate for at least six months without new billings coming in. But no firm should ever let things reach that point.

As I wrote in *Collecting Your Fees: Getting Paid from Intake to Invoice* (ABA, 2003): "Law firms are not the victims of their delinquent clients. You and the firm itself cause your collection problems by not telling clients from the beginning what you expect from them, and continuing to follow through. Thus you and your firm are the only ones who can solve your collection problems." That still, and always will, hold true. The solution is always in your hands. And the best solution for any lawyer is to make sure clients know that they must pay their bills, on time and in full.

"Making good decisions is a crucial skill at every level."

–Peter Drucker

Section 15:

Getting More Information

Additional information relating to law firm fees, collections, and compensation is voluminous. The following selection of resources is not an attempt to be comprehensive, but it does indicate the types of sources available to readers seeking more detailed background and analysis on the issues.

Firm Compensation Statistics

The *National Law Journal (www.nlj.com)* has annual supplements titled "What Lawyers Earn," and *Of Counsel: The Legal Practice and Management Report* (Aspen Publishers) does an annual survey of lawyer and paralegal salaries. *Corporate Counsel* conducts annual surveys of general counsel salaries.

Also, the *American Lawyer* compiles the annual AmLaw 100 list, which includes law firm profits per partner.

Information on law firm compensation at all levels is published in IOMA's *Compensation & Benefits for Law Offices.*

On the Web, FindLaw's "Firm Salary" page posts associate salaries *(www.infirmation.com/shared/insider/payscale.tcl)* and many legal newspapers report on salaries for their state or city in their online versions. The Vault organization *(www.vault.com)* has become the gospel among associates for compensation and other law firm information.

In addition, the National Association for Law Placement (NALP) publishes the one-volume *Associate Salary Survey,* broken out by location, employer size, type of employer, and other categories. A summary of the survey is posted on the NALP Web site *(www.nalp.org).*

Also, the Association of Legal Administrators (ALA) publishes a one-volume *Compensation and Benefits Survey* covering law firm staff.

Consulting Resources

Legal industry consulting organizations offer extensive survey information that relates to law firm financial performance and client perceptions of value and service. Here are primary ones.

- **Altman Weil, Inc. (www.altmanweil.com)** regularly conducts surveys of attorney and staff compensation and analyzes performance measures for firms of all sizes.

- **The BTI Consulting Group (www.bticonsulting. com)** annually benchmarks client service performance and various budgeting and financial metrics for law firms.

- **Hildebrandt International (www.hildebrandt.com)** provides in-depth analyses (more conceptual than statistical) on compensation and performance.

- **IOMA (Institute of Management & Administration, www.ioma.com)** publishes the flagship *Law Office Management & Administration Report*, which focuses on keeping private law firms profitable and successful. An annual highlight is the exclusive survey of law firm administrators and managing partners published each December. The comprehensive survey covers all the areas that leaders need to make sound management decisions at the end of the fiscal year. Other publishing, research, training, and audioconference services focus on law firm compensation.

American Bar Association Publications

The ABA has a number of relevant books and reports, with the following being particularly helpful.

- *Compensation Plans for Law Firms,* 4th Edition, by John D. Cotterman (2004). Complete and systematic guidance on establishing a workable compensation plan, including good information on what firms use and avoid.

- *How to Draft Bills Clients Rush to Pay,* 2nd Edition, by J. Harris Morgan and Jay G. Foonberg (2003). Advice on how to prepare bills that satisfy clients and make them more likely to pay.

- *Results-Oriented Financial Management: A Step-by-Step Guide to Law Firm Profitability,* 2nd Edition, by James G. Iezzi (2003). Tips on improving financial systems, including preparing and analyzing budgets.

- *Unbundling Legal Services: A Guide to Delivering Legal Service a la Carte* by Forrest S. Mosten (2000). Covers the practice of offering discrete services from a menu of offerings.

- *Winning Alternatives to the Billable Hour: Strategies That Work,* 2nd Edition, by James A. Calloway and Mark A. Robertson (2002). How to initiate and implement different billing methods that make sense for firms and clients, including how to explain—clearly and persuasively—the economic and client service advantages in changing billing methods.

- *Billing Innovations: Win-Win Ways to End Hourly Billing* by Richard C. Reed (1996). An older but comprehensive look at most of the various alternative billing concepts and techniques.

Fee Agreement Forms

These volumes provide helpful pointers and examples.

- *Attorneys' Fees*, 3rd Edition, by Robert L. Rossi, Thomson West. This two-volume discussion of attorneys' fees includes an appendix with sample agreements.

- *The Essential Formbook: Comprehensive Management Tools for Lawyers* by Gary A. Munneke and Anthony E. Davis, ABA. Volume 1 includes client intake and fee agreements. Volume 2 covers fees, billing, and collections.

- *Fee Agreement Forms Manual*, 2nd Edition, Continuing Education of the Bar, California. Although emphasis is for the California Bar, sample provisions may provide guidance in creating an agreement appropriate for other states. Also contains commentary, sample agreements, and a checklist of sample provisions and addresses ethical issues.

- *Fee Agreements for Virginia Lawyers*, Dennis M. Ryan, Editor. Another state-specific guide with many examples that can be adapted for other jurisdictions.

- "Sample Engagement Letters and Fee Agreements," P.A. Henrichsen, ABA *GPSolo* magazine, January/February 2007.

Weblogs

A number of bloggers who focus on the legal profession (or blawgers, to use the term of art) write extensively on fee and compensation issues. These are three of the most notable ones.

- **the[non] billable hour, www.thenonbillablehour. typepad.com.** Matthew Homann shares inventive and original ways to bring meaningful and satisfying change to the practice of law. His blog focuses on how innovative billing strategies, creative marketing techniques, cutting-edge ideas from other industries and professions, and proven customer service principles can combine to improve the ways lawyers serve their clients.

- **Adam Smith, Esq., www.bmacewen.com.** Lawyer, businessman, and consultant Bruce MacEwen focuses this publication on improving the economics and management of law firms. He provides both statistical analyses and general discussions and focuses on AmLaw 100 firms.

- **Law Department Management, http://lawdepartmentmanagement.typepad.com.** Rees Morrison is a certified management consultant who has advised law departments for nearly 20 years to help them better manage themselves and their outside counsel. A former practicing lawyer, author of six books, a senior director of Hildebrandt International, and a prolific blogger, Rees offers insightful and provocative ideas about the way corporate counsel select law firms.

LawBiz® Management Company Resources

The LawBiz® Management Company of Edward Poll & Associates, Inc., at *www.lawbiz.com,* is a leading consultant organization that works with lawyers to increase their profits and their effectiveness at practicing law. Mr. Poll is a nationally recognized coach and adviser who gives coaching and strategic guidance to national and regional law firms and their leaders on practice management, business development, and financial matters.

He has written what has become the standard guidebook to improving the law firm collections function: *Collecting Your Fee: Getting Paid From Intake to Invoice* (ABA, 2003). In addition to its text analysis, the book has a CD-ROM that contains forms for intake, engagement letters, status reports, budgeting, sample bills and collection letters, accounts receivable aging reports, and more. In addition, he maintains a Weblog at *www.lawbizblog.com.* He is widely recognized as one of the most prolific and insightful blawgers on issues related to law firm finances, management, and operations. His blog contains an archive of posts on these general issues (including compensation and collections), and it has substantial links to other blawgs and materials.

Mr. Poll frequently writes and speaks on "The Business of Law®," and his other widely praised books, which are all detailed on and available through his Web site, *www.lawbiz.com*, include the following volumes:

- *Attorney and Law Firm Guide to the Business of Law: Planning and Operating for Survival and Growth*, 2nd Edition (American Bar Association, 2002). A comprehensive guide to all aspects of operating a law firm.

- *Business Competency for Lawyers: A LawBiz® Management Special Report.* The A to Z essentials of making more profitable decisions in every part of your law business.

- *Disaster Preparedness & Recovery Planning for Law Firms: A LawBiz® Management Special Report.* How to develop a comprehensive response and recovery strategy to ensure your firm's survival in the face of disasters of many types and sizes.

- *The Profitable Law Office Handbook: Attorney's Guide to Successful Business Planning.* A best-selling practical guide that enables attorneys to take control of their financial futures.

- *Secrets of The Business of Law®: Successful Practices for Increasing Your Profits.* Specific suggestions for greater operating efficiency and profitable revenue generation.

- *MORE Secrets of The Business of Law®: Ways to Be More Effective, Efficient, and Profitable.* New hands-on tips and tactics for successful practice management, client relations, and much more.

- ▶ *Selling Your Law Practice: The Profitable Exit Strategy.* The leading authority in this field, a guide to help attorneys determine the value of their law practice and get top dollar for it.

- ▶ *The Successful Lawyer-Banker Relationship: A LawBiz® Management Special Report.* What you need to know to build and strengthen a solid banking connection to ensure your firm's foundation and growth.

- ▶ *The Best of Law Practice Management Review: The Audio Magazine for Busy Attorneys™.* One-hour audiotapes presenting expert interviews on the latest law practice management techniques.

For updates on topics covered in these books, as well as information and analysis on the latest trends in law firm business management, visit *www. lawbizblog.com*—cited as one of the 50 top legal blogs by TechnoLawyer and 100 best blawgs by the *ABA Journal.* And get LawBiz® podcasts at *www.lawbiz. com/podcasts.html.*

Receive your complimentary subscription at *www.lawbiztips.com.*

Appendix

Sample Engagement Letter Fee Provisions

State Bar of California Fee Provisions Examples

Following are sample attorney-client fee agreements prepared by the Committee on Mandatory Fee Arbitration of the State Bar of California and approved by the Board of Governors. They are advisory only. They are not binding upon the courts, the State Bar of California, its Board of Governors, any persons or tribunals charged with regulatory responsibility, or any member of the State Bar.

These agreement forms are designed for use in non-contingent fee arrangements. They cover (1) litigation on an hourly basis and (2) a contingency fee matter. Except for those references specifically relating to trial practice, the litigation example could also be used for a non-litigation matter. Included here are only those provisions specifically detailing the fee provisions for the matter.

Litigation – Hourly Arrangements

1. SCOPE OF SERVICES. Client hires Attorney to provide legal services in the following matter: [describe matter]. Attorney will provide those legal services reasonably required to represent the Client. Attorney will take reasonable steps to keep the Client informed of progress and to respond to the Client's inquiries. If a court action is filed, Attorney will represent the Client through trial and post-trial motions. This Agreement does not cover representation on appeal or in execution proceedings after judgment. Separate arrangements must be agreed to for those services.

2. CLIENT'S DUTIES. Client agrees to be truthful with Attorney, to cooperate, to keep Attorney informed of any information or developments which may come to the Client's attention, to abide by this agreement, to pay Attorney's bills on time, and to keep Attorney advised of the Client's address, telephone number, and whereabouts. Client will assist Attorney in providing necessary information and documents and will appear when necessary at legal proceedings.

3. DEPOSIT. Client agrees to pay Attorney an initial deposit of $ [amount] by [date]. The hourly charges will be charged against the deposit. The initial deposit, as well as any future deposit, will be held in a trust account. Client authorizes Attorney to use that fund to pay the fees and other charges as they are incurred. Payments from the fund will be made upon remittance to client of a billing statement. Client acknowledges that the deposit is not an estimate of total fees and costs, but merely an advance for security.

Whenever the deposit is exhausted, Attorney reserves the right to demand further deposits, each up to a maximum of $ [amount] before a trial or arbitration date is set. Once a trial or arbitration date is set, Client shall pay all sums then owing and deposit the attorneys' fees estimated to be incurred in preparing for and completing the trial or arbitration, as well as the jury fees or arbitration fees, expert witness fees, and other costs likely to be assessed. Those sums may exceed the maximum deposit. Client agrees to pay all deposits after the initial deposit within [number of] days of Attorney's demand. Unless otherwise agreed in writing, any unused deposit at the conclusion of Attorney's services will be refunded.

4. LEGAL FEES AND BILLING PRACTICES. Client agrees to pay by the hour at Attorney's prevailing rates for all time spent on Client's matter by Attorney's legal personnel.

Current hourly rates for legal personnel are as follows:

Senior partners	_____	/ hour
Partners	_____	/ hour
Associates	_____	/ hour
Paralegals	_____	/ hour
Law clerks	_____	/ hour

The rates on this schedule are subject to change on 30 days' written notice to Client. If Client declines to pay increased rates, Attorney will have the right to withdraw as attorney for Client. The time charged will include the time Attorney spends on telephone calls relating to Client's matter, including calls with Client, witnesses, opposing counsel, or court personnel. The legal personnel assigned to Client's matter may confer among themselves about the matter, as required and appropriate. When they do confer, each person will charge for the time expended, as long as the work done is reasonably necessary and not duplicative. Likewise, if more than one of the legal personnel attends a meeting, court hearing or other proceeding, each will charge for the time spent. Attorney will charge for waiting time in court and elsewhere and for travel time, both local and out of town. Time is charged in minimum units of one-tenth (.1) of an hour.

5. COSTS AND OTHER CHARGES.

(a) Attorney will incur various costs and expenses in performing legal services under this Agreement. Client agrees to pay for all costs, disbursements, and expenses in addition to the hourly fees. The costs and expenses commonly include service of process charges, filing fees, court and deposition reporters' fees, jury fees, notary fees, deposition costs, long-distance telephone charges, messenger and other delivery fees, postage, photocopying and other reproduction costs, travel costs including parking, mileage, transportation, meals and hotel costs, investigation expenses, consultants' fees, expert witness, professional, mediator, arbitrator and/or special master fees, and other similar items.

(b) Out-of-town travel. Client agrees to pay transportation, meals, lodging, and all other costs of any necessary out-of-town travel by Attorney's personnel. Client will also be charged the hourly rates for the time legal personnel spend traveling.

(c) Experts, Consultants, and Investigators. To aid in the preparation or presentation of Client's case, it may become necessary to hire expert witnesses, consultants, or investigators. Client agrees to pay such fees and charges. Attorney will select any expert witnesses, consultants, or investigators to be hired, and Client will be informed of persons chosen and their charges. Additionally, Client understands that if the matter proceeds to court action or arbitration, Client may be required to pay fees and/or costs to other parties in the action. Any such payment will be entirely the responsibility of Client.

6. BILLING STATEMENTS. Attorney will send Client periodic statements for fees and costs incurred. Each statement will be payable within [number of] days of its mailing date. Client may request a statement at intervals of no less than 30 days. If Client so requests, Attorney will provide one within 10 days. The statements shall include the amount, rate, basis of calculation, or other method of determination of the fees and costs, which costs will be clearly identified by item and amount.

Contingency Arrangements

1. SCOPE OF SERVICES. Client is hiring Attorney to represent Client in the matter of Client's claims against [name, and possibly others as future investigation may indicate], arising out of [matter], which occurred on or about [date]. If a court action is filed, Attorney will represent Client until a settlement or judgment, by way of arbitration or trial, is reached. Attorney will oppose any motion for a new trial or any other post-trial motions filed by an opposing party, or will make any appropriate post-trial motions on Client's behalf. After judgment, Attorney will not represent Client on any appeal, or in any proceeding to execute on the judgment, unless Client and Attorney agree that Attorney will provide such services and also agree upon additional fees, if any, to be paid to Attorney for such services. Services in any matter not described above will require a separate written agreement.

2. RESPONSIBILITIES OF THE PARTIES. Attorney will provide those legal services reasonably required to represent Client in prosecuting the claims described above and will take reasonable steps to keep Client informed of progress and developments, and to respond promptly to inquiries and communications. Client agrees to be truthful with Attorney, to cooperate, to keep Attorney informed of any information and developments which may come to Client's attention, to abide by this Agreement, to pay Attorney's bills for costs on time, and to keep Attorney advised of Client's address, telephone number, and whereabouts. Client agrees to appear at all legal proceedings when Attorney deems it necessary, and generally to cooperate fully with Attorney in all matters related to the preparation and presentation of Client's claims.

3. LEGAL FEES. Attorney will only be compensated for legal services rendered if a recovery is obtained for Client. If no recovery is obtained, Client will be obligated to pay only for costs, disbursements and expenses, as described below. The fee to be paid to Attorney will be a percentage of the "net recovery," depending on the stage at which the settlement or judgment is reached. The term "net recovery" means: (1) the total of all amounts received by settlement, arbitration award or judgment, including any award of attorneys fees, (2) minus all costs and disbursements set forth in Paragraph 6. [Net recovery shall also include the reasonable value of any non-monetary proceeds.] Attorney's fee shall be calculated as follows:

(i) If the matter is resolved before filing a lawsuit or formal initiation of proceedings, then Attorney's fee will be X percent (X%) of the net recovery;

(ii) If the matter is resolved prior to [number of] days before the date initially set for the trial or arbitration of the matter, then Attorney's fee will be X percent (X%) of the net recovery;

(iii) If the matter is resolved after the times set forth in (i) and (ii), above, then Attorney's fee will be X percent (X %) of the net recovery.

In the event of Attorney's discharge or withdrawal, Client agrees that, upon payment of the settlement, arbitration award, or judgment in Client's favor in this matter, Attorney shall be entitled to be paid by Client a reasonable fee for the legal services provided. Such fee shall be determined by considering the following factors: (1) The actual number of hours expended by Attorney in performing legal services for Client; (2) Attorney's hourly rates; (3) The extent to which Attorney's services have contributed to the result obtained; (4) The amount of the fee in proportion to the value of the services performed; (5) The amount of recovery obtained; (6) Time limitations imposed on Attorney by Client or by the circumstances; and (7) The experience, reputation, and ability of personnel performing the services.

4. NEGOTIABILITY OF FEES. The rates set forth above are not set by law, but are negotiable between an attorney and client.

5. COSTS AND LITIGATION EXPENSES. Attorney will incur various costs and expenses in performing legal services under this Agreement. Client agrees to pay for all costs, disbursements, and expenses paid or owed by Client in connection with this matter, or which have been advanced by Attorney on Client's behalf and which have not been previously paid or reimbursed to Attorney. Costs, disbursements and litigation expenses commonly include court fees, jury fees, service of process charges, court and deposition reporters' fees, photocopying and reproduction costs, notary fees, long-distance telephone charges, messenger and other delivery fees, postage, deposition costs, travel costs including parking, mileage, transportation, meals and hotel costs, investigation expenses, consultant, expert witness, professional mediator, arbitrator and/or special master fees, and other similar items.

Client understands that a deposit for costs may be required before the expenditure is made by Attorney. To aid in the preparation or presentation of Client's case, it may become necessary to hire expert witnesses, consultants, or investigators. Attorney will select any expert witnesses, consultants, or investigators to be hired, and Client will be informed of persons chosen and their charges. Client authorizes Attorney to incur all reasonable costs and to hire any investigators, consultants, or expert witnesses reasonably necessary in Attorney's judgment unless one or both of the clauses below are initialed by Attorney.

Attorney shall obtain Client's consent before incurring any costs in excess of $ [amount]. Attorney shall obtain Client's consent before retaining outside investigators, consultants, or expert witnesses. If an award of fees and/or costs is sought on Client's behalf in this action, Client understands

152

that the amount which the court may order as fees and/or costs is the amount the court believes the party is entitled to recover, and does not determine what fees and/or costs Attorney is entitled to charge Client or that only the fees and/or costs which were allowed were reasonable. Client agrees that, whether or not attorneys' fees or costs are awarded by the court in Client's case, Client will remain responsible for the payment, in full, of all attorneys' fees and costs in accordance with this Agreement.

Additionally, Client understands that if Client's case proceeds to court action or arbitration, Client may be required to pay fees and/or costs to other parties in the action. Any such award will be entirely the responsibility of Client.

6. DEPOSIT. Client agrees to pay Attorney an initial deposit for costs of $ [amount], to be returned with this signed Agreement. Attorney will hold this initial deposit in a trust account. Client hereby authorizes Attorney to use that deposit to pay the costs, disbursements, and other expenses incurred under this Agreement. When Client's deposit is exhausted, Attorney reserves the right to demand further deposits, each up to a maximum of $ [amount]. Once a trial or arbitration date is set, Attorney will require Client to pay all sums then owing, and to deposit the costs Attorney estimates will be incurred in preparing for and completing the trial or arbitration, as well as the jury fees or arbitration fees likely to be assessed. Those sums may exceed the maximum deposit. Client agrees to pay all deposits required under this Agreement within 10 days of Attorney's demand. Any deposit that is unused at the conclusion of Attorney's services will be refunded.

7. MONTHLY BILLING STATEMENTS. Attorney will send Client monthly billing statements for costs, disbursements, and expenses incurred in connection with this matter. Each statement is to be paid in full within 15 days after the date of such statement.

A General Letter Example

The two preceding examples from the State Bar of California are obviously very formal and legalistic documents. An engagement letter can be informal and still set forth the fee terms explicitly. The following example is such a document.

Client Name
Client Street Address
City, State, Zip Code

This letter will confirm our understanding that, upon your signature, you have retained [name of law firm] to represent you in [describe matter], and we agreed to [insert relevant details].

Before proceeding with this legal work, the firm requires a deposit and initial retainer of $____.

Attached to this letter is a listing of lawyers in our firm who may work on your matter and their corresponding current rates/fees. Charges are made for all professional services connected with your matter, including in-person and telephone conferences. In addition to fees for professional services, the firm bills for out-of-pocket expenses we may incur, including, but not limited to, long-distance telephone charges, photocopying costs, postage, mileage in accordance with current Internal Revenue Service standards, filing and recording fees, and the like. As we discussed in our conference, we will advise you before undertaking any procedures that will substantially increase the fees that will be necessary to properly represent you in your matter.

Our bills are normally prepared and mailed within a few days of the beginning of each month. **All bills are due and payable upon receipt.**

If bills are not paid when due, the firm reserves the right to discontinue legal service and to withdraw from representing you as a client. However, we will not discontinue service without giving you notice of our intention. In the event of the firm's withdrawal, we will mail a certified letter to your last known address. Upon receipt of your written request and payment of any necessary shipping costs, all your papers and property in the firm's possession will be returned to you.

We look forward to working with you.

Sincerely yours,

_____

[Law Firm by Lawyer in charge of client relationship]

Agreement and Acceptance:

I agree to the above terms and conditions.

_____

Client

Dated: _____

Get these other informative books by Ed Poll

Disaster Preparedness & Recovery Planning for Law Firms
By Edward Poll

It isn't a question of if your firm will face a disaster but *when* it will. How will you and your people respond? Disaster planning is one of the most specialized, most overlooked, and most vital business planning endeavors. The goal is to develop a recovery strategy to get your firm up and running again and thus ensure its survival. This volume gives you the critical steps, including:

* The essentials of a comprehensive recovery plan
* How to create a team to plan the firm's response
* Where legal ethics and disaster planning intersect
* Must-dos to safeguard and support your people

MORE Secrets of The Business of Law®
By Edward Poll

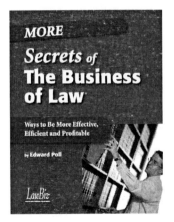

In this follow-up companion volume to Ed Poll's highly praised first *Secrets* collection, you'll learn how to be even more efficient, more effective and more profitable in your practice. You'll get topflight tips for how to:

* Collaborate with clients
* Succeed in collecting your fees
* Maximize the return on your technology investment
* Make the most of outsourcing services
* Exceed your clients' expectations
* Fine-tune disaster and recovery planning
* Open your own law office
* Raise your rates
* Build a Weblog strategy
* And a whole lot more

Attorney and Law Firm Guide to
The Business of Law:

Planning and Operating for Survival and Growth, Second Edition
By Edward Poll

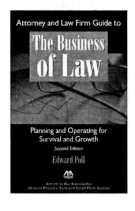

Do you want to:
* Be more successful by design than by accident?
* Be more profitable?
* Attract more clients?
* Have your clients pay on time?
* Have greater control of your practice?
* Have greater peace of mind?

If your answer is yes to any one of these questions, you must read this book. Ed Poll had simplified the mystical process of operating a law practice so anyone can be more effective with his or her clients and become more profitable.

Selling Your Law Practice:
The Profitable Exit Strategy
By Edward Poll

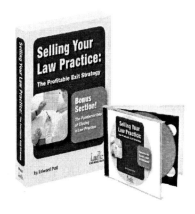

Get Top Dollar for Your Law Practice!

You will discover how to:
* Determine the value of your practice
* Set your sale price
* Evaluate and describe your practice's unique characteristics
* Negotiate the sale more effectively
* Anticipate transition issues
* Review state's Rules of Professional Conduct for selling a practice

The accompanying CD contains the sample contracts, forms, and financial worksheets from the book in Word and Excel format!

Call (800) 837-5880 or visit www.lawbiz.com to order!